D0905285

Moving Spirits, Building Lives

THE CHURCH MUSICIAN AS TRANSFORMATIONAL LEADER!

HUGH

BALLOU

Library of Congress
Control Number 2005905004

ISBN 0-9772148-0-X

First printing   July 2005
Second printing   April 2006

Supplements to this book are available online at
http://www.hughballou.com

Printed in the U. S.A by
Morris Publishing
3212 East Highway 30
Kearney, NE 68847
1-800-650-7888

TABLE OF CONTENTS

ACKNOWLEDGEMENTS

It is an honor to recognize all those who have contributed to my learning process in my forty years on a church staff, mostly as Director of Music. It is also frightening to recognize any particular person for fear of leaving someone out who has played a major role my journey of discovery. Some friends and mentors have helped create a major paradigm shift, maybe without being fully aware of their impact on my thinking process. Others have created challenges for me to solve, which have helped me to grow. Finally, there are those who have seen me fail and have continued to believe in my gifts and determination to succeed. Not giving up has been my response to those countless individuals who have given much to me over time.

Those whom I wish to thank personally are, first, the ones who help proof and edit the manuscript for this book. They are A. J. Ballou, Kay Shirley, Fonda Martin and Diana Calhoun Bell. Thanks to my colleague, Shane Kennedy, who helped with the book title. Thanks to Tedi Ballou for her support for 30 of these years. There are many, many others who have shared insights with me over the years. Some of them are: Dick Schultz, Bob Summer, Jerry Black, Art Ross, and Larry Dill, each of whom had a unique influence on my journey of personal growth and learning. Thanks to Herb Krutoy for his graphic design work.

This journey of writing a book was inspired and assisted in a brainstorming session with Dean McIntyre and Dan Benedict at the United Methodist Church General Board of Discipleship in Nashville, Tennessee.

There are also many others who have contributed and are way too numerous to mention without leaving out one of them.

God has richly blessed me with resources, the most valuable of which is an abundance of great friends who share their knowledge freely with me. Thanks to all of you.

PREFACE

In this book, Hugh Ballou offers an inspirational and practical guide to competence and excellence in church leadership. A winsome leader and experienced facilitator who has demonstrated his skill in a wide variety of situations, Hugh combines theory with practice to suggest clear steps for the leader who truly desires to break out of the pack and strive for the exquisite beauty of a job well done.

Beginning now and extending into the foreseeable future, effective worship must be created in teams. Experience in several high demand congregations have prepared Hugh to be a worthy advisor to those who aspire to move from the isolation and dullness of traditional methods to the excitement and energy of new possibilities.

Work with yourself using the prompts in this little book. You will not be disappointed!

Dr. Larry Dill
Executive Director
The Institute for Clergy Excellence
Huntsville, Alabama

INTRODUCTION

Moving Spirits – Building Lives is about transforming lives through the various ministries of today's church. It is, however, very focused on the position of the church musician. God calls the church musician and those skilled in ministry through music, not as an end in itself, but as a means to a greater end – forming Christian faith through all we do.

Being or becoming a church musician is a very different identity and skill set than a musician doing church music. There really is a tremendous difference! The church musician -- the conductor of the choir, the music leader for worship -- must be focused on and dedicated to leading people in a strong spiritual journey through liturgy and worship participation. It is a unique and very special duty and delight! The conductor is, in fact, a spiritual leader, a transformational leader empowered by God.

Examine the word *Transform*. It does not merely mean change, or we would use that word. It is a verb with an expanded vision and is much more transcendent. It implies a deeper, more fundamental alteration of our very form (to *trans – form*). The continuing process of transformation begins with the moment of inspiration and continues in us through times of action, rest, and reflection. The conductor is in a unique position to affect and change lives positively for the faith journey. Music directors are a fine-tuned instrument for God's use.

The assumption in writing this book is: 1) the musician is one of the valuable resources to a senior minister, and 2) this relationship can amplify the effectiveness of the total ministry. In this book, I attempt to help ministers and musicians understand the steps in becoming Transformational Leaders by injecting group dynamics into every part of ministries they touch.

If you consider the choral ensemble, which we call "the choir" as the perfect example of transformation, then you have the concept. A group of people show up as individuals to sing in a rehearsal.

They each have unique gifts and qualities. It is the job of the conductor to form an ensemble, a unique community, which, in a synergistic way, accomplishes much more than any individual or group of individuals can accomplish. The concept is transformation: Transforming individuals into community musically. The process of transformation does not stop with the musical result; it becomes part of a faith journey for individuals as well as the community.

The church musician is in a very unique position, indeed. There is power to transform and empower people's lives not only on a weekly basis, but also on the long faith journey throughout life. The most important results of faith renewal are not measurable in conventional or immediately available methods. These results are realized many times over long periods of time, even over an entire lifetime.

I'm offering "life experience" education to complement the "facts only" idealistic education attained from the educational institution. Many musicians graduate from the same school and move into a typical church music career, their practical experience will change the way they do the things they were taught. And in many cases, their ways may contradict what they were taught. Each experience can be unique. This is a compilation of what I learned over forty years of teaching, learning, listening, watching, etc. Some lessons were learned the hard way, and some were dodged bullets. The insights of this book will lead the dedicated music ministry professional to a path of greater fulfillment.

My personal faith statement inspires me to feel the way I do about worship.
The church is intended to be the word of God lived out, a community of faith, the body of Christ, and the family of God. In unity of faith and commonness of purpose, Christians are called to worship, learn, practice, and strengthen their faith so they may be equipped as Jesus' ambassadors in the world. The church also plays an indispensable role in the spiritual nurturing, of God's people.

Worship, and liturgy are ways we experience the presence of God as a community of believers. Music is liturgy. Music is a spiritual medium, without which worship is incomplete. Music is God's gift to us and is complete when used to praise God, our creator. Through worship, I can be myself unconditionally and feel loved by God unconditionally.

My purpose for writing this book

This book is an offering to those who struggle with the unique situations that arise in trying to do the Lord's work in the environment called the church. I have often said the fiercest test of one's Christian faith comes with being called to serve on a church staff; whether full-time or part-time status. The work is the same, only the pay changes. Actually, there's no such thing as being part-time on a church staff. It requires a total commitment. Part-time church work is like being partially pregnant.

This book is a compilation of wisdom I have been fortunate to acquire over thirty-eight years of work on a church staff. Principles and ideas have grown out of constant struggle and failure in the midst of wonderful success and joy. There is nothing new here, only a collection of ideas and principles that have been helpful to me over the years. I have learned a little from everyone I have encountered along the way, and a lot from those unique individuals to whom God has given much and to whom God has given the opportunity to share much. I give credit to all these incredible people who have come into my life to offer their experience and wisdom, both helpful and challenging.

The other body of wisdom, which is endless, is the collective knowledge found in writings by those who want to share their experiences as well. It's there in the libraries and bookstores, but not tapped by most. Most of us want to simply try things on our own and then fail. Statistics show only 3% of those reading this or any other source will actually do much about it.

The personal crises that finally lead me to collect these thoughts arose out of my calling to a ministry where the solutions to stress seemed to be ever elusive and most frustrating. The following situations were especially taxing:

- Constantly feeling there is vastly too much to do and not enough time to do it
- An unclear understanding of what my responsibilities were as a leader, not just a choral director
- Entering an out-of-control situation with virtually no experienced help in getting up-to-speed in the new job
- Having to solve situations faster than my understanding of ways to deal with them
- Balancing my time to work everything in, such as
  o Pastoral issues
  o Music planning
  o Recruiting, assimilating, and retaining new volunteers
  o Being able to spend time with large numbers of volunteers
  o Implementing my plans
  o Follow-up with important details
  o Conflict resolution

Working through these challenges led me to review what I know about leadership in the church and helped me to realize others might just have some of the same problems. As I worked through formulating an action plan to get things on the right track, I realized I had a book to publish.

Consider tidbits of wisdom like the selections at the world's best produce market. Not all of us will pick the same fruit. We pick the one we think is best, the one we think works best to satisfy our hunger.

I have learned a lot, but my greatest lessons come with trying to teach others. I humbly offer this collection. I hope others will find some new directions in the pages to follow.

My process of transformation

A running story

I have personal experiences of transformation both within and outside of the church. One of my most profound experiences of transformation was becoming a successful runner. It was more than a hobby, however. It was a process of transforming my body and spirit. Running is not something that comes easy to me. In fact, it is quite difficult!

When I decided to begin, I was not very fit. I had not been active or skilled in any athletic activity. So, I decided to run. It looked like it would be easy, and I didn't need a lot of equipment.

So I started. I began at my driveway. I would run around my neighborhood. I could be a runner and compete in races like the people I've seen running around town!

Well, I could barely make it from one driveway to the next. What a chore it was! I thought I could never do it.

I went to the bookstore and bought a book about running. I just knew there was a secret I was missing. It was the spirit of encouragement! I was inspired! The writer was very encouraging. He suggested running some and walking some. So, I did it. I made it past two driveways!

Over the next month I got a little better each day, and at the end of five weeks, I could make it a whole mile! How great that was! The next goal was two miles. It took about three months to make it to the two-mile mark without stopping to rest or walking a part of the way. I wanted to run the whole way. And I did!

What next? Add another mile. And I did. Without stopping. It took another month to get to that point. It was worth it! I had accomplished a major goal and lost some weight. AND, I felt much better, not only physically fit, but also emotionally fit.

I found out the difference in a "jogger" and a "runner" is a race entry form.

So, I decided to enter a 5K-road race. It was in Dunedin, Florida. I remember the day quite well. I was very intimidated by all those "runners." They all appeared to know just what they were doing, and I had no idea what was ahead.

I paid the registration fee, got my number, pinned it onto my shirt, and waited for the starting gun. (I arrived ninety minutes early, so I had plenty of time to focus and get nervous.)

The time came to line up. I moved into place with all those "experts." And we waited.

At last, it was time to begin. The starter moved into place and described the routes. He wished us good luck, and pulled the trigger of the starting gun.

We were off. It was off to a new adventure for me.

There weren't a lot of hills in Dunedin, Florida, but there were bridges to get over. If you are not a great athlete, a small rise in the terrain is noticed. So, I was struggling up the rise in the road over a bridge at my ripe old age of forty-eight and a young mother pushing a stroller with twins zoomed past me. How humiliating!

Next, a gentleman in his mid seventies moved next to me and would obviously pass me as well. I asked if he had been running long. He replied (as he was passing me) that he had run all his life, but was faster before he had had knee joint replacements. He moved on.

Well, that made me feel like I was not as fit as I might have hoped. But, I continued to run. I wanted to finish. I wanted to finish without stopping. I wanted not to finish last. I accomplished both of those goals.

I went home and looked in the local newspaper for club listings. I found a running club that met on Tuesday afternoons. So, I showed up the next week at their training run.

I met the coach. I told him I wanted to sign up for the running program and join the club. He looked at my shoes and shorts and advised me to update both. I had no idea what he meant. So, I went to a local sports store and made some purchases. Now, I was a runner. He gave me a training plan tailored for my age and ability, and I was off to a new phase in this life adventure.

I moved to Atlanta to take a new position and joined a group there, the Leukemia Association's Team In Training. I signed up to run the Atlanta half-marathon. The commitment was not only to train and run, but to also raise money for Leukemia patients.

I ran the half-marathon. I did not stop at all. I did not finish last. In fact, I was in the middle of the pack of 7,000 runners. I had come a long way – from one driveway to the next to the completion of a 13.1-mile race.

This is a story of transformation: transformation of body; transformation of will power; transformation of spirit; transformation of life goals. It was not that I ran a long road race. It was the fact I had set a high goal, worked toward that goal systematically, and met the standards I had set for myself. I was transformed into a new body shape as well as into a new emotional being. I became a person who knew success.

My perspective on a musical ensemble as transformation
Conductors understand transformation experientially. The very nature of our work is that of transformation.

A group of singers shows up for rehearsal. They come to sing – each with a different perspective and possibly a different level of talent. The skilled choral conductor listens, instructs, motivates, encourages, and affirms the changes necessary to mold this unrelated group of singers into a unified sound. The product is called an *ensemble*. We strive for that unity as an ensemble each time we rehearse or perform.

The magic of transformation is absolutely necessary in the world of music. Transformation happens not by chance but also by intention, not only from the leader, but from the participants as well. The results are cumulative. Once the sense of ensemble is achieved and experienced first hand, it can be believed.

So why are we not committed to building that sense of ensemble in all we undertake? Maybe it's an education issue for those whom we lead. Maybe it's a lack of understanding that this is a transferable concept from musical groups to other groups.

Why is that concept so foreign to all of us? And why does the concept seem unattainable? We can believe in the universal power of transformation. Are we willing to try? Are we willing to teach?

My success story

In at least three churches while serving as Director of Music Ministry or Director of Worship and Fine Arts, I have tried these strategies, resulting in synergistic solutions to every day problems. If you are interested in establishing a "MEGA-program," regardless of the size church, then this book will give you some empowerment to reach that goal. Regardless of the church membership and regardless of the mood of the church and regardless of a weak Sunday attendance record, YOU CAN FILL IT UP FOR SPECIAL EVENTS! These events will give energy and momentum to the whole church and all its ministries. Be the catalyst! Be the visionary! Be the one who excites the community with passion! Establish processes to take you there.

My latest incredible experience is at Trinity United Methodist Church in Huntsville, Alabama. It's a wonderful, small city with a highly educated population. When I arrived, the programs were good, the choir was excellent, the worship services were powerful, but the energy and attendance were uneven. The contemporary and traditional musicians were not working together, and, generally speaking, there was not a general sense of team spirit among worship services, various ministries, or staff members. So, we created a team spirit among all the players and powerful outreach musical programs.

- Concerts that constantly fill the auditorium or sanctuary long before their beginning
- Worship attendance that doubled over a few years
- Worshippers who attend both contemporary and traditional services
- Ministry departments that partner to bring increased effectiveness to programs
- Partnerships with community concert organizations that bring cash flow and large numbers of visitors
- Ministry programs that interface with and relate to all worship services

How? Well, that's the focus of the book. Please read on….

The organization of the book

The book is organized into five sections of instruction, examples, visions, and questions to stretch your imagination. These are followed by one section to challenge and envision an unlimited future. The resources in each appendix will give you forms and outlines to lead you into new adventures.

Section One provides the foundation information for mapping success with chapters on the following:

- constructing vision and purpose statements,
- defining the identity of your ministry,
- finding a path to excellence in all you do,
- setting powerful, but attainable goals.

The sooner you realize the value of daily planning and evaluation, the sooner you can begin moving on the path to achievement. The section shows how to build the foundation and how to begin forming good habits that will shape your life and ministry.

Section Two gives insight into the dynamics of relationships. No church program should be undertaken without collaboration.

Those around you, member and staff, are needed in the journey which leads to a successful result. Learn to share; learn to help; learn to let go and get out of the way when necessary. The journey is as important as the result. The journey is the main thing; it will greatly impact the result – for good or for bad! It's all a part of God's plan. Be open to these relationships! Distribute the wealth! Share the success!

Sections Three and Four brings into focus those God-given talents that develop the community. You are a *Transformational Leader!* Your very presence and influence empower others to grow, to learn, and to give. Do not underestimate your influence - both good and bad. So, learn about influence and use it for God's glory!

The chapters in this section help you master the following leadership skills:

- Accomplishing what you plan
- Successfully promoting all your programs
- Running meetings that empower teams to go beyond their expectations
- Running meetings that are fun and that people actually want to attend
- Focusing on being a professional - all the time!
- Understanding how you influence the flock to grow spiritually

Section Five is called "What Now" because it is now up to you to succeed. However, there are some ideas of direction and resources for your consideration.

It is up to you. Find your passion and go for it without losing even one day. Napoleon Hill developed a leadership strategy from interviews with the most successful leaders of his day, including people like Thomas Edison, Henry Ford, Harvey Firestone, and many others. In his groundbreaking 1937 classic motivational book, *Think and Grow Rich*, Hill summarized his leadership philosophy with one sentence: "Whatever the mind can perceive and believe can be achieved." He also listed the thirteen traits of wealth. Here are just a few of them: ability for applied faith, a positive mental attitude, a pleasing personality, and good physical health. The very last attribute on Hill's list is the ability to attract money. Money, important as it is, is the least important of true wealth attributes. So, why not set your mind on a higher level of achievement right now and go forward with that plan? You transform lives through bringing excellence to all you do. Do all you do for the glory of God, who is the giver of all gifts and talents.

May God bless not only your successes, but also bless your journey. Don't just seek to arrive at the destination of success. Enjoy the journey. It is the process that makes the difference!

SECTION 1

Understanding Your Calling

Ordinary people believe only in the possible.
Extraordinary people visualize
not what is possible or probable,
but rather what is impossible.
And by visualizing the impossible,
they begin to see it as possible.

Cherie Carter-Scott

Transformation begins within the soul and spirit of the leader. Learning to identify ways to center your very being is the first step in becoming a transformational leader.

You must learn to look inward and discover your true identity and your essential gifts before attempting to impact the lives of other people.

This section will guide you in learning to discover your inner self and working out of that understanding to impact the world around you. **Be you - share with others.**

1. Vision and Purpose

Know why God has given you this talent

Leadership is the capacity to translate vision into reality.

Warren G. Bennis

Management is efficiency in climbing the ladder of success; leadership determines whether the ladder is leaning against the right wall.

Stephen R. Covey

The transformation process begins with a vision of becoming. What to become is the issue. Know why you are doing what you do. Every moment of life is precious. Decide what is important and waste no time in moving forward with an action plan, moving you toward those most important realizations. Some of the opportunities will only be present for a brief time and may only present themselves once. Be ready. I like the phrase "success is when preparation meets opportunity." It is worth repeating: **Be ready.**

Make a master list of your reasons for choosing music ministry

List all the reasons you can think of for choosing music ministry as a vocation or avocation. List them on a piece of paper or on 3x5 index cards. Be as specific as you can, but keep it brief. You are not writing an essay or justifying your choice; you are defining your motives.

Look at the list. Place the index cards on flat surface such as a table and move the ideas together that relate in some way. If there are several cards in each location that relate, then give the category a name. Maybe *Teaching Biblical Lessons* is a possible category. Maybe *Making Great Music* is another. You get the idea.

Arrange the cards in order of preference or importance. Discard cards that are unimportant or insignificant. You might only be able to discard ideas after listing all the ideas you can create, then comparing them all. This might help set priorities for where you are and where you will put your effort and time.

Once the categories are defined, combine the individual statements, making a statement inclusive of all cards.

Review the categories and final statements and see if your calling is defined. See if this defines how you use the majority of your time. See if these statements are supported by your ministry outcome. See if your work reflects your calling.

Once you have defined your reasons for choosing ministry, see if you can determine whether or not your own personal needs are manifested through your work goals. See if your calling is a personal fulfillment. See if you can identify ways successful ministry outcome is personally fulfilling.

Write your own vision and mission statement

Vision Statement
Take the statements you created and develop a personal vision statement. Why are you doing ministry? What difference is your work making to those whom you lead? What is the difference your work makes in quality of programming, quality of work environment, and quality of relationships? Understand your vision for your work as a church leader taking on the task of transformational leadership.

What is your personal vision statement? What is your vision? Have you considered just what it is that you are all about? What insights has God given you for your days on earth? What will you do about it?

Your personal vision statement is what you want. Moreover, it is about what you can create out of yourself and the world as you see it. It is about how much more you can succeed than you had ever imagined. What turns you on? Your passion is what will drive and inspire you to success. Your joy will be in your successful journey on the path defined by your vision statement.

Think about joyful moments during the past week, during the past month, and so on. What are they all about? Can you summarize how you felt about them and how they inspired you to want to do more? Did you create joy for someone else? Did you create joy for some group or organization? Maybe you created joy for your congregation or your choir or study group. Write down the feelings you remember about those situations. Can you identify what direction to proceed in order to do more of the same?

Can you identify which of these projects or successful accomplishments were achievements that took you above the level you expected? Can they be identified as excellent? Is excellence your passion?

Keep a journal. After all, if your life is worth living and is important, isn't it worth recording? As you journal, remember to record your feelings, not just your accomplishments. How did you feel when you gave joy to someone? How did you feel when you achieved something you would classify as excellent? How did you feel when you went the extra amount to impact your future or the future of a program or another person? Are the feelings an inspiration to you? Remember these feelings. Recall the feelings when the going gets tough in the future. Successful people have positive images to recall that empower them when life is tough or when resistance seems too much to bear.

Read your journal entries and make note of the key factors that will inspire you and help you articulate your vision for your future. Remember to focus not only on work accomplishments, but focus on health, recreation, and artistic items as well. If you are creative and if you are healthy, you will be more in tune with God's world around you.

Create a template or worksheet for defining your vision statement. After all, you will revise this statement often. God lets us grow from life, and thus our vision changes when we get to a new place. Constantly read and revise how your vision statement is worded, and maybe you will have to start all over as your priorities change.

Your worksheet or template should have guiding statements followed by lots of white space to use to respond to the statements. Maybe those statements are simple statements followed by words to guide your thinking.

The first part of this guide sheet is a section to identify your values. What is it that God has put into your heart? What do you believe? So the first section is about your values – your beliefs. Knowing what you believe keeps you on track. If you don't stay on a consistent path with what your core values are, then you will not be happy. Your core values define who you are.

So, the first section will tell you what you are about. Try making a list of words to guide your thinking in this section. They will guide your actions, set up your philosophy, and drive your strategic planning process for your life.

Section one: Key Values and Core Beliefs (I believe, I value, I appreciate, I know, etc.)

Section two is going to help you construct the vision statement. First, list what motivates you. Look at your notes from your journal. Then, inventory your skills. Don't try to concentrate on what is most difficult for you. Capitalize on your main skill set, and then identify what steps to take immediately. Don't worry about knowing everything about what you will do. Just know what to do first. Know how you can start. Start today!

From these guiding principles, begin to write your statement. Make it complete, but not too long. A 30-word vision statement is enough. Use strong verbs to lead your thinking. What words inspire action? Use words like EMPOWER, ENABLE, INSPIRE, DEVELOP, CREATE, and DELIVER. Make your list. Make the verbs strong ones will open up your thinking to "out of the box" thinking. You want to be bold in order to get somewhere you have not been before.

Now write it! Read it! Sleep on it! Read it again! Share it! Live it! Do not be afraid! Be bold (write that word, too!)

Your vision statement should tell anyone interested, and some who are not, just who you are and what you are about. This will lead you to developing a mission statement.

Here is a sample of a vision statement: *To constantly provide an environment for myself and others to live out their faith journey, growing in God's grace and improving service to others.*

Try yours!

My Vision Statement:

Mission Statement

Once the vision is defined, develop a mission statement. The vision is the concept; the mission statement is its application. It is a statement of purpose and function. Your mission is what you will do. If you believe everyone should get along, then your mission is peace. If you believe in creating new experiences for faith journeys, then your mission is about meaningful programming. This mission statement portrays how it looks when you get there, or your purpose. It comes from your belief statements.

Mission statements should be concise and to the point. Resist the temptation to make it too long.

A sample mission statement could be something like this: *I will be a transformational leader by planning and implementing programs that allow for pastoral concern and personal growth of each participant through effective content, inclusive structure, and joyful attitude.*

Now, go for it!

> ### *My Mission Statement:*
>
>
>
>
>
>

Guiding Principles
Remember listing your core values? Turn those into guiding principles and make a list. Put this list, with the vision and mission statements, along with the action plan, which will consist of goals and objectives. These guiding principles will help you remember how to implement your plan.

Guiding principles might look like this:
- *Every person has value in some program and can contribute according to his or her ability. I recognize the value of each contribution.*
- *I will stay current on my skills by reading and attending to my continuing education.*
- *I will balance my life with work and rest, with focus time and recreation, with good sound diet and regular exercise.*

- *Every thing I schedule is of importance; otherwise I will not give it time.*

Your Action Plan
Your action plan is two-fold. First write your goals, and then write your action plan to achieve those goals. Action plans consist of specific objectives or tasks, when they will be accomplished, and just how you will do them. The next chapter will guide you in the goal setting process.

Summary Notes
Make a resource guide for success. Include in this guide a structure for implementation. Include the following:
1. Devices for control – calendar, PDA, notebook, etc.
2. Resource of inspirational quotes (include key scriptures)
3. A methodology or philosophy for implementation (read goals daily, study scriptures daily, review journal weekly, share plans with someone who will hold you accountable, etc.). This will ensure your daily walk toward success.
4. Commit the plan to God's care and trust in God's supporting strength and grace
5. Review plans on a regular schedule (quarterly, semi-annually, etc.) and prune, revise, and redirect as necessary.
6. Relate each step and each action to your goal of being a transformational leader

A note to the weary and frantic: You are most likely thinking by now that this whole thing is too laborious, too meticulous, and too time consuming when you can't get things done as it is! NEVER FEAR! ALL IS WELL! If you take time here to plan, you will save an enormous amount of time by not floundering and having to make up for lost time. So – **DO IT!**

My Core Values

My Vision

My Mission

2. Goals

Know EXACTLY where you are going.

> *If you do not know where you are going,*
> *every road will get you nowhere.*

Henry Kissinger

> *Great things are not done by impulse,*
> *but by a series of small things brought together.*

Vincent Van Gogh

Setting goals is a fundamental success principle, especially for the Transformational Leader. Goals are written down. Unwritten goals are merely dreams. No one experiences the full potential of his or her abilities without setting specific, written, timed goals. A principal factor that makes goals work is the principle of accountability. Sharing goals builds group synergy, group advocacy, and accountability. That works!

Be careful what you set as a goal in life. It's not what you achieve that matters most. It's what happens to you and others as you attain the goal.

Now we move to setting goals. Try it. It will enrich your life. First, let's define goals.

Goals are SMART
S = Specific
M = Measurable
A = Accountable
R = Realistic
T = Timed

You can find these principles in just about every book on leadership or success. Writing goals is essential for success. In *The Seven Habits of Highly Effective People*, Stephen R. Covey outlines and teaches his success principles. The one relevant here is "Begin with the end in mind." If you are planning a trip, you know where you will end up, that is, if you plan a trip to Paris, France, then you will know when you arrive you have been successful in your goal. If you arrive in Paris, Texas, you might want to reevaluate your planning skills!

The point here is to be very specific when writing your goals. I have included a resource for writing goals in the appendix, which will help you in this part of your journey to success (See Appendix I: Goals Worksheet). Writing and accomplishing goals is transformational not only in your life, but also in the lives of those you lead and those with whom you work.

In one church where I served as Director of Music, I brought a complete set of goals for myself and for the music ministry to a three-day ministry staff planning retreat. I distributed copies to the other members of the team as I took my turn in sharing about the upcoming programs. The room was very quiet. They were reading the details of my goals and taking notes. There were a few questions, polite questions, and then we moved on with the agenda. The next time we were at a similar retreat, everyone had goals to share. I was affirmed! The bar was raised in that everyone saw value in something that I had brought to the table. I was certainly glad that I had had the courage to share these important goals with the team. It was not only a good idea to share the goals in order to inspire the other staff members (not my intention at all), but it was a good experience for me to make myself vulnerable.

Vulnerability is where growth happens and creativity is free to be expressed. As we make ourselves vulnerable, others are likely to respond. This is not only true in making music, but in numerous other areas as well.

I am talking about personal goals here, not team goals. Both are important and both are valuable. Share your personal goals and make yourself accountable. That will make a difference in your achievement. Also, explore department or team goals with your colleagues. There's great strength in combining talents and visions for greater strength.

The real reason to share goals is so they are achieved! Yes, being vulnerable is essential. You must be willing to share goals openly with colleagues. This will fulfill the accountability part of goals. The other side of that issue is that you have partners in helping you achieve your goal. Yes, sharing your specific goals lets others know just what you want to achieve, and they will help you get there – willingly or unwillingly, consciously or unconsciously. They will have become part of your support group.

The goals I shared in that staff retreat were all successful, even ones that I did not have time to implement. It is a mystery, but sharing openly and honestly is a principle that works. We are afraid to share specific goals because of a fear of failure to meet the expectations lined out in the goals. Therefore, ensure that what you write for your goal is realistic and attainable.

We are also afraid to write down and commit to specific goals because we might fall a little short. So, if you say you want to have 100 singers in a specific choir by a certain date and you end up with 95, have you failed? More importantly, are you a failure? NO! The guiding principle here is that you have achieved success. Maybe you have increased the choir significantly with quality voices and willing volunteers who will assist in other ways. You have achieved your goal of increasing the choir's numbers and bringing energy and quality to the group.

It is what happens to you and your team as a result of your goal that is most important – not the exact result of each goal!
The anonymous quote at the beginning of this chapter encourages you to set worthy goals. What happens to you and your group is the most important result of your goal. You could certainly bring in

lots of bodies to join the choir who can't carry a tune or have rotten attitudes. This is not the result you desire. While you may want to improve the musical quality of the choir and the number of people is related, but is not the final issue.

Focus on the key factors when setting your goals. What is most important? Who will be affected? What benefit will the group receive? What relationships will be built or strengthened? What difference will you make in the lives of the people you lead?

Let's go through the key factors that make a worthy goal:

S=Specific
Specificity for goals is crucial. Set your sight on a specific target or targets. You won't know if you succeed unless you define what success looks like.

Here are some examples that illustrate vague and specific goals:

Vague: To increase the size of the Sanctuary Choir.

Specific: To build energy in the Sanctuary Choir by increasing the membership by 10% to 100 members who will add quality and harmony to the mutual ministry of the ensemble. Completion date: December 1, 2006 (1 year of elapsed time).

Vague: To increase the number of volunteers in music ministry.

Specific: To build efficiency in administrative parts of the music ministry by inviting and empowering 10 new members in ministry to participate in an area of their passion, interest, and skill. Completion date: January 30, 2007 (2 years of elapsed time).

Vague: To inventory and catalogue the sheet music library.

Specific: To design and implement a system for cataloging the sheet music library, which will provide identification on the file boxes to match the computer records. Completion date: May 30, 2007 (1½ years of elapsed time).

Do you get the idea? I have given examples of several goal principles – specific, timed, measurable, and realistic. The missing element is accountability.

Specificity is not only in the attainable quantity, but also in the type of result. What is the benefit for this goal? Spell it out.

M=Measurable

How much is enough? What is the "critical mass" or "critical amount?" Unfortunately we must measure some things in an environment where the most important accomplishments are not measurable – person, faith, growth, salvation, sanctification, relationship with God, etc. We count numbers, but the things that matter the most cannot be counted.

So, why do we set measurable goals? These numbers are validation for achievement. These achievements set up the successes we cannot measure. The programs we produce and the music we offer are not the final blessing. However, these are the tools God uses to guide us on our faith journey. After all, if we just sat around waiting for God to move us, we would not be faithful to scripture. *And he said unto them, Go ye into all the world, and preach the gospel to every creature.* Mark 16:15

Know what the end looks like. Visualize the result. Begin immediately to work toward your goal. Do not wait until you are fully ready. If you wait to be ready, then you will never get started. The quantifiable result is a motivating and clarifying factor. If you have taken time to fully think through each goal and its benefit, then you will know when you arrive. Make it measurable so there is no doubt when you arrive. By the way, the timing of reaching goals is not an accurate science. It is purely a guess. Therefore, you might get to your result long before you planned to get there. If that happens, then make new goals and keep on striving for excellence!

A=Accountable

Sharing your goals with someone who will hold you accountable is a key secret for achieving your goals. A good person to share them with is someone who can hold your feet to the fire. Share your goals and stay in touch with that person. Not only will that relationship keep you accountable, but that person, in his or her own way, will propel you, or even assist you, in attaining that goal.

Accountability is also community. When you are willing to be vulnerable, you invite the participation and empathetic support of others. Sharing invites participation, either active or inactive.

Napoleon Hill, in his book *Think and Grow Rich,* gives many examples of "mastermind" group. This is another type of accountability and advocacy support. Regular meetings of this team will help you pool the best thinking skills of each member and the result is greater than the sum of the parts. In fact, this is the definition of synergy that Covey uses in his writings. When you can combine skilled thinking and customize the output to solve your life challenges, then you are one step ahead of others who are just trying to keep up.

The individuals in your thinking and resource group can be people of like mind from similar professions or people with different goals but similar leadership principles. You can also choose a variety of folks from different professions who have different work styles. Your group must, however, be made up of people whom you trust and with whom you can share your innermost thoughts. It is essential that each member of the group be successful and seek to be more successful – people whom you want to be around and would like to emulate. They must also believe that one can harness the combined spiritual force to focus spiritual energy on the prescribed goal. *For where two or three are gathered together in my name, there am I in the midst of them.* Matthew 18:20

It works something like this:
- Choose people you respect – learn from those who are successful.
- Set the size of the group – 4 to 6 is ideal; there is time for everyone to interact.

- Meet on a regular basis – weekly or bi-monthly, but often enough to do some good.
- Set the length of the meeting – one hour works unless there is a meal.
- Begin with prayer – invite God's participation and seek his blessing and guidance.
- Set a schedule that allows time for each person to share – stick to it.
- Each person should talk – share good and bad.
- Each person should listen and respond to others.
- Allow time for group interaction – brainstorm, evaluate, strategize.
- Appoint a process person to keep time and monitor participation.
- Ensure that each member is committed to the common goal.
- Challenge each other to stretch because of this group.
- End with prayer – thank God for the blessings received and those yet to come.

Choose a group of people who have similar aspirations. If you are interested in development, choose real estate people. If you are interested in investing, choose people with strong financial skills. If you are interested in business… well, you get the idea.

Make your list of prospects; call them in order of preference. Stop when you have a large enough group to begin. Set your sights high. Choose people who are successful and with whom you wish to associate. After all, transformation begins with a vision. Choose someone who has seen and fulfilled a vision. Transformational Leaders begin with transforming their own lives.

Set a time to meet that will work for everyone and stick to it. Set a time line for how long the group will exist and then dissolve the group at the end of that time or recommit to another schedule of meetings. Begin on time, end on time, and keep your schedule. However, life does not offer us challenges in equal doses or in precise time allotments that are the same. If someone in the group has a large problem or major concern to share with the group, then begin the meeting by requesting time from other members. If you negotiate 1 or 2 minutes with several others, then you can have extra time to work on a special need.

This is accountability in high gear! It may not be your style. Push yourself to get out of your comfort zone and share your goals. You will be an inspiration to others.

R=Realistic

Set your sights on something attainable (some strategists use this word for the A in SMART). It is very frustrating and most disheartening to continually miss your mark when trying to reach your goals.

Realistic also means worthy. Why are you choosing the particular goal? What difference will it make in people's lives? What difference will it make to your life?

Remember, what happens to you and to those whom you lead is the real benefit of setting and sharing goals, not just the stated purpose. As you approach the goal-visioning process, take a look at the overall picture. Remember to look at your list of core values and the core values of your organization. Realistic goals are goals that will make a difference in the organization, its programs, and its people.

Realistic goals are transformational goals. I've created a sample checklist for sorting the realistic factors for goals. Maybe you will use this list the first time you work on your next set of goals, but you will most likely make your own list.

Here are some ways to define "Realistic" when setting goals:
- Is the outcome consistent with the culture of this organization?
- Will the impact on other people and programs be perceived as beneficial to all?

- Is there enough time for the process to fully develop and be understood by all?
- Is the number of anticipated supporters greater than the expected critics?
- Is it actually possible to accomplish the defined outcome?
- Should this goal be divided into several more practical steps?
- Do I really, really believe in the value of this goal?
- Do I really, really believe that this goal is attainable?

That may be too long a list for you; however, you can develop your "hot list" of evaluators for checking the reality of your vision.

T=Timed

Timed means you have a specific ending date for your goal. You've stated what it will look like when you get there; now state when you will arrive. Use the trip analogy again. If you are traveling from St. Petersburg, Florida to St. Louis, Missouri, you most likely will use a map and maybe even the services of a trip planner who will give you not only the best route, but also the time needed for the journey.

This is the final, but the not least important, factor for your goal process. It is also the factor that contributes heavily to the failure of most goals. Failure comes from not setting clear time frames for accomplishments. Failure comes from setting the goal and the time to be accomplished, carefully filing the goal sheet away, and remembering two weeks before the deadline that you have committed to a project or idea.

You will be successful in making your thoughts and dreams manifest themselves into physical form by setting timed objectives for short-term benchmarks. These benchmarks remind you of your long-term vision, affirming the reality of your vision and its progress.

Here's the secret for achievement: break your goal into small, measurable, timed, benchmarks or objectives. When setting bold, wide-spanning visions and claiming bold ambitions, then it is good for you and your team to have measurable steps for realizing and celebrating success along the way. These baby steps, when realized, will propel you and your team forward on your transformational journey. Remember, ask yourself if you accomplish a goal without having changed anything or anybody or having improved anyone's life or enjoyment, then what was the value of setting that goal? The words of Covey ring true: *"Begin with the end in mind."*

Be the Transformational Leader! Be bold and commit to your visions for excellence! Don't just believe that you can make a difference, KNOW that you will make a difference!

A note to the weary and frantic: This process of goal setting is very intimidating! It is very difficult to get to the place that it is comfortable exposing your innermost thoughts and dreams without fear of failure or ridicule. Goal setting is a powerful transformational process, not only for you but also for your team. **So – DO IT!**

3. Excellence

Take time to prepare properly; no dull music!

"A phrase is inevitable." Robert Shaw

"Body, mind, spirit, voice, it takes the whole person to sing and rejoice." Helen Kemp

"Music did not reveal all of its secrets to just one person." Attributed to Ralph Vaughan Williams

"Don't make so much sound that you can't move it around." Joseph Flummerfelt

"Every syllable has integrity." Fred Waring

"Never sing louder than beautiful." René Clausen

"Conducting is the act of making manifest that which we have heard inside our heads." René Clausen

This chapter deals with the challenge of making the musical performances the very best they can be. Far too much music is considered to be dull, when, in fact, it is the performing of the music that is dull. The church musician commonly deals with unskilled volunteers who need to be taught almost everything repeatedly. They also need to be motivated weekly to continue the path to excellence. The transformational process here is inspiring and motivating to volunteer musicians.

Consider choir rehearsal a teaching opportunity. Educated singers and knowledgeable worshippers are more involved, more active, better prepared, and get more out of each experience. Do not lecture. Work on incorporating educational moments into the flow of your rehearsal plan. Add related facts to appropriate places as notes are fixed or interpretation added or changed. If people understand why the music was written (understanding the text) or why a certain text is appropriate for the particular occasion, then they will respond with more commitment in their participation.

Know your craft

The most obvious place and the place that shows the most immediate result of being a Transformational Leader is in the area of choral music. It's short and simple – the choral director is a Transformational Leader. The choral director takes a collection of unrelated people who sing and transforms the group into a choral ensemble. The effectiveness of this job is immediately measurable and quite evident. Choral directors are evaluated constantly. We are only as good as our last performance. Paintings and sculptures can stay on exhibit eternally, but music disappears. We only have our memories or our recordings to duplicate the experience again.

Understand vocal music if you are a choral person, but not a singer. Learn what good vocal technique is and learn how to teach others. Think about the physical implications of the music you choose and the challenge to your choir in learning and performing the selected anthems or songs. Know how much time it will take to teach the music. Knowing how long it will take to teach the notes is one thing. Getting a group to make music is quite a different challenge. Your influence in teaching the ensemble what that difference is makes the experience transformational. It is the key factor. Any choir can sing notes. Only the exceptional ones make music.

Create a positive learning environment

Our physical surroundings make a significant difference in how we feel. How we feel makes a significant difference in how well we learn. The physical surroundings are comprised of the look and feel of the room, how good the sight lines are, how well everyone can hear him or herself and each other, and how the mood of the rehearsal is positioned. Learning is fun. More can be learned if it is fun. More can be learned if it is clear what is expected and what the current activity is supposed to be. Use visual reinforcement for what is spoken. Professional educators know that we retain 10% of what we hear, 20% of what we see and 60-80% of what we see, hear and do. Music teachers know that adding a kinesthetic element to the learning experience increases the learning experience.

Here are some ideas:
- Post the rehearsal music in large letters in rehearsal order
- Have all the music readily available
- Identify ways to communicate details
  - Use a white board
  - Use an overhead projector
  - Use chart pads

Be clear about all expectations and have everything organized. Time needs to be spent on singing, not on undoing confusion.

Have a clear idea of how every part of the music is expected to sound. Know what you want and mark it in your music. Be definite and be clear and be concise. **They didn't come to choir rehearsal to hear you talk – they came to sing!** Get to the point, tell them what you want, and then let them sing it. If you correct a difficult place, let them sing it over. Repeat it until it is solid. Practice it correctly to undo the incorrect image that exists.

Keep the rehearsal energized by keeping it moving. Know what comes next by knowing your rehearsal plan thoroughly. Have the singers arrange their music in rehearsal order so that you don't spend time announcing what piece comes next and then having to wait while everyone finds the correct piece of music. Establish a rhythm for the rehearsal. Momentum creates its own energy. This doesn't mean that the pace needs to be brisk for the entire rehearsal. It means that the rehearsal should flow from one item to another without dead time. Slow down the pace from time to time with a story, a joke, or a learning moment. Intersperse non-singing activities into the rehearsal to allow for time off from singing constantly. This is especially important if the rehearsal is 2 hours long. That's a lot of singing if there is no time to rest.

Have pencils readily available for marking the music. Explain what it means to "mark your music." Not everyone is up to speed on every term we use. When asking volunteers to mark certain things in their music, always explain why and exactly what you mean by marking the music. Draw an example of what you expect them to mark on your board or overhead transparency so they can understand. Don't lose people because they don't understand and are afraid to look silly to others by asking a question.

Use effective communication skills
When you stop the choir, have a specific reason and explain it. Tell them what was wrong and how to fix it. Then let them try to sing it correctly. If you talk, then have something worth saying.

Know why you want them to sing the selection and when it will be sung. Know the text and know how to explain it. Then do it. If you do not talk about the text, then some people will never, ever connect with the text and its meaning. After all, the text is usually what inspired the composer to write the music. Choral music springs from the text. Know what that means. Know how to communicate it. Be concise.

Know where the group is in their musical knowledge and communicate on that level. Don't talk down to anyone. Just know how to explain what you want in terms they will understand. Demonstrate the desired result. Check to see if they fully understand before continuing to sing anything incorrectly. Be attentive to what is happening in the rehearsal.

Basically, always strive to inspire musical singing, not just singing of the notes. Teaching volunteer choral groups to sing musically is a constant challenge and a constant blessing. Here is another transformational experience: transform notes into meaningful, emotionally fulfilling sound. Encourage musical development with every phrase and throughout every musical selection. Constantly strive for excellence. No more dull music!

Learn to be vulnerable

In *The Musician's Soul*, James Jordan writes about being vulnerable in front of the choir in order to let them sing and to make beautiful music. You will not be able inspire great musical singing until you are able to be vulnerable in front of the group. If you are guarded in sharing yourself, they will respond accordingly. If you are inadequate in being expressive, they will be flat as well. Open up your emotional self to allow them to do the same. Look beyond the notes to the essence of the creation in front of you. Don't look at the sheet of music; look at your singers. Don't yell at them for not looking at you when you don't look at them. Get them on board by communicating your enthusiasm!

Be passionate about your music making. There is only a small percentage of the population who can sing and make music. It is a very special gift indeed. Treat it as such.

A note to the weary and frantic: Don't take this gift of making music lightly. This is a spiritual gift that will enrich your life, the life of those whom you lead and the lives of those to whom you sing. There is but one chance to get it right. It is your duty and delight to do it well. So – **DO IT!**

SECTION 2

Relationships are Transformational

The most important ingredient we put into any relationship is not what we say or what we do, but what we are. And if our words and our actions come from superficial human relations techniques (the Personality Ethic) rather that from our own inner core (the Character Ethic), others will sense that duplicity. We simply won't be able to create and sustain the foundation necessary for effective interdependence.

Stephen R. Covey

This section defines the essential elements in developing and maintaining relationships that are at the heart of ministry - all ministry.

4. The Minister/Musician Dynamic

Know and respect your roles

> *Take the first step in faith.*
> *You don't have to see the whole staircase,*
> *just take the first step.*
>
> Martin Luther King

This chapter deals with the principle relationship in church ministry – the relationship between the minister and musician. It is crucial that this relationship be the best it can possibly be. It is all too often a major source of conflict in the church. Transformational leadership begins at the top. **Set the standard. Set the pace. Set the example.**

The Relationship

The key working relationship and the heart of worship leadership is the relationship between the senior pastor and the director of music. Setting the standard for this relationship will be setting the standard for others to follow – even the entire church! After all, if the two people leading the organization cannot work in harmony, how then will they be able to lead others to do so? In order to lead in worship and to inspire a congregation to work together in unity, this relationship must be the model.

Get to know each other. Maybe even share scores from an instrument such as Myers-Briggs or Birkman. Know how the other person wants to be treated. A bad idea is to follow the "Golden Rule." The principle in that rule is to treat others as you would like to be treated. Wrong! Treat others as *they* would like to be treated. Yes, we might want to be treated differently than someone else in our group wants to be treated. So be it!

When sharing feelings and preferred working styles, be honest. Tell the other person just how you feel. Get to the point and don't waste time beating around the bush. Get on with life and don't waste a single minute by being unclear or indirect.

Do something else together besides work. Also, find ways to show the other person that you care. Think about ways that can be affirming, not only of the things that relate to work responsibilities, but also the things of a personal nature. People want to be appreciated not only for what they accomplish, but also for who they are personally. In fact, being appreciated is reciprocal in the work world as well as personally.

Be honest about feelings and perspectives without robbing the other person of his or her own feelings. It is okay to disagree with your supervisor, as long as you are not threatening. Understanding the other person's point of view is the first priority; only after you understand one another can you explore differences of opinion. Your personal relationship must be firm. It only works if both parties have permission to disagree. It only works if the musician fully acknowledges that the minister has the final say in decisions. It only works if there is an earned trust in the relationship. However, this is an excellent way for each person to know how the other thinks. It is also an excellent way to explore strategies for problem solving.

In order to work in an honest relationship, you must establish a strong level of trust. That means not doing anything that will destroy the trust of the other person. That means not making unilateral decisions that should involve the other person unless the terms of decision-making have been arranged. That means the trust level is strong enough that each one of you knows the other person always intends to do the right thing. It also means that when there is a departure from trusting behavior, intentional or unintentional, the offending party must come clean and deal with the issue openly and honestly. This means an apology and then, take a step to rectify whatever damage has been done.

Give a wide berth for the other person in times of major stress. Be "in tune" when things are going wrong in his or her life. Show again, that you care.

Understand your roles

The senior minister is in charge. Period. All the duties and responsibilities of the musician are a delegation of the minister's responsibilities. Having said that, the minister should not micromanage the musical details that are your responsibility. If things are not as you expected, then take steps to move in a different direction.

One of the areas of great tension in worship planning is the choice of music. The minister wants to mold the worship experience to fit a certain vision. The musician has a vision as well. It is essential that the minister communicates the vision of the final result and then gives time for the musician to develop that vision. It might take time. There needs to be progress along the way. There must be a demonstration of intent with visual acknowledgement in some way.

On the other hand, the musician needs the tools and resources to pull off the vision. The Transformational Leader knows and embraces a clear vision. The Transformational Leader knows and embraces the value of change, not just for the sake of change itself. The Transformational Leader knows that communication of this vision to the worshipping community at large will help transform the experience for everyone. Having stated all of those facts, it is essential that the minister give the musician the tools and resources to accomplish the desired task. The musician must clearly identify what those tools and resources might be. One very, very important item is lead-time.

Lead-time for getting a choir prepared for a particular piece of music can be quite extensive. The reason this part of ministry is delegated to a professional is to get the job done. Therefore, asking for a particular song or anthem for a given Sunday during the previous week is not reasonable and demonstrates a lack of understanding. Lead-time for the choral musician usually is about 4 to 8 weeks. Here are the elements that must precede a successful choral presentation:

- Understanding the text or message to be supported
- Researching resources to find the appropriate piece of music
  - Correct text
  - Good musical value
  - Pleasing to the choir and congregation
  - Singable by the choir
  - A piece that sounds good when sung by that particular choir
  - Time to order and receive the music
  - Time to learn the music

The variables in the structure above differ greatly. It is, however, the generally accepted norm. Times will arise when a piece must be learned during the weekly rehearsal and presented on Sunday with only one rehearsal. If this becomes the norm, then the quality of the music will suffer greatly, as will the attitude of the participants. Both choir and congregation will sense the lack of "music" when songs or anthems are constantly presented for worship before they have been fully digested by those leading the music.

It is of utmost importance that the musician feels understanding and support from a minister who wants the best worship experience for everyone. Deciding what model should be the norm and deciding what the strategy should be when the norm cannot be attained are the crucial steps here.

Another area where personal relationships are stretched and sometimes harmed is when sensitive things are spoken to each other in a place that is not private. Take special caution in expressing comments that are sensitive, and ensure that they are delivered only in person and only in private and only in a sincere way. This means these messages are not delivered in notes, through email, and especially not through a third person.

Never, Never, Never Triangulate!

There are many books on this subject. Read some. In the meantime, speak directly with each other. If there is some action that the other person has done to offend you, tell them. DO NOT tell anyone else. The only secret that is confidential is the one you don't tell anyone. Once you tell anybody a confidential item, it is no longer confidential. It will leak out without your knowledge and harm the relationship.

Think about how you would feel, and maybe have felt, when a negative comment about you comes to you from a third party. You have no way to respond, especially if that person says this to you in "confidence." Solve the problem. Don't triangulate.

If a third person comes to you with negative information about another person, ESPECIALLY about your senior minister, do not get involved. If the information is already relayed to you before you can stop it, then refer that person to the minister directly. Usually, they will not tell the person with whom they are upset. This is particularly true if they have just released all the negative energy onto you. The most effective strategy is to say that you will have the minister call them. You cannot agree to accept this communication as confidential. It is unfair for a person to speak to you and then claim that the comment should have been confidential. Do not agree. You did not agree to receive the information in confidence and you do not need to let this person control you in a negative manner and put you in a compromising position. It will help that person to tell the minister how he or she feels directly. This is an opportunity for ministry and it is an opportunity for you to demonstrate and earn the trust from your minister.

Accepting negative information about a third person when that person is not present is triangulation. If someone attempts to relay negative information to you about another person, stop it as soon as this is evident. Offer the following options: 1) may I have "Xxx" contact you? 2) ask if they have spoken to that person directly 3) refuse to listen 4) refuse to keep the information confidential, or 5) diffuse the situation in another way of your choice.

Have a regular time to "Check-in" with each other
It is actually nice to have time to work out all the necessary details. That special time becomes dedicated to just this working relationship. It becomes a time to look forward to where you both will deal with important issues and feelings. It is really nice to have your special time together. Cherish the time, and use it wisely. Establish a firm time and place to "check-in" with each other.

Always play fair
Develop an understanding about what this means. There are some areas to think about, such as agreeing to communicate and agreeing on how much to communicate. Ensure that there are no surprises to leave one of you off balance. Arrive for your meetings having completed the assigned tasks, being fully informed on projects, and generally being prepared to the time ahead. Listen carefully. Know who's in charge and don't challenge decisions inappropriately. Clearly state your feelings, but remain flexible. Always act in a professional manner. Negotiate the necessary changes relative to previous decisions, but abide by the final decision.

Do all you can do to ensure that this is the best working relationship it can be. It will pay off for both parties.

A note to the weary and frantic: You might think there is not sufficient time to get the job done, much less to do all it takes to build a strong relationship here. Spend the time and invest in this relationship. Transformation cannot happen without it. Ever! So – **DO IT!**

5. The Staff as a Team

Learn to network with colleagues

> *Anyone who loves his opinions*
> *more than his teammates*
> *will advance his opinions*
> *and set back his teammates.*
>
> John C. Maxwell

Many, many churches have so many programs that it is impossible for every staff member to keep up with or even participate in every program. At best, keeping up with every program is difficult, if not impossible. However, there are many programs that should not be produced by only one staff member or even one department. If you adopt the concept that no church program can stand alone, then explore how to make every program more effective, more enjoyable, and more easily executed by combining forces with colleagues in the planning and execution of programming. Set a standard with your team and reach out to other teams to connect all the parts.

Knowing about individuals and knowing who they are can transform how they are perceived and received. Build in time to get acquainted, even with people whom you already know. There's always more to them. We live in a culture that defines us by what job we have and what we own, not by who we are personally.

Set the standard

In his book *The Five Dysfunctions of a Team,* Patrick Lencioni defines the five dysfunctions as:

1. Absence of Trust
2. Fear of Conflict
3. Lack of Commitment
4. Avoidance of Accountability
5. Inattention to Results

Items #1 and #4 are the most prevalent in church settings, with #5 coming in a close third place. Absence of trust is the team killer! Often, we do not know how to deal with it openly and honestly in the church setting. Many of us feel as though Christians must always be kind and caring; therefore, we do not challenge others when there is evidence of indirect, passive-aggressive, or dishonest behavior. The Transformational Leader must "speak the truth in love" and challenge members of the team when the behaviors occur. Conversely, the Transformational Leader must be willing to respond to similar requests for clarity and declaration of intent.

Building trust and accountability among team members is essential to the success of the team. The process of clarifying these team standards for how members of the team will relate to each other is important. These expectations cannot be assumed. A list of guidelines must be established, made available to every member, and posted for each team gathering. The guidelines are set by the team, modified by the team and clarified by the team – continually. This, in a sense, is a "Covenant Agreement" for the life of the team and/or the team's project.

It may appear to be a waste of time to define what seems like obvious standards; however, in establishing these standards, some members may find disagreement about others' accepted standards. In fact, the process of identifying and defining these guidelines will help the team learn new ways to create a safe environment for brainstorming, clarifying, sorting, and eliminating information. The way the team relates, operates, and functions defines how strong it will be and how solid its planning process will be. The process itself builds trust, builds community, and builds momentum. Basically, if the team's processes are flawed, then the team's output is likely to be flawed as well.

Deal directly with the issues of trust and accountability. Define what those terms mean in your context and what the expectations will be for those items. Set expectations for following the standards, and set expectations for when they are not followed. This means that each person must feel comfortable enough in the environment to disagree with others. It means that conflicting perspectives must be allowed. It means that members of the team will learn from each other. It means that nobody gets his or her own agenda satisfied, but the group gets their agenda satisfied. It means that consensus is not always agreeing. Consensus is working together to define the group's opinion.

My thesaurus lists the following words as some synonyms for *consensus*: agreement, accord, harmony, compromise, and consent. Consensus is possibly a combination of all of those. Make up your team's own definition, post it, and use it to build synergy.

Over and over again, teams discover new ideas and new freedom as they define their standards. This is an excellent way to learn how team members think and respond to each other. Set a time frame for this discussion and don't let it continue unnecessarily long. Don't rush the process, either. Taking time to do this step will save time and aggravation later.

Ensure that everyone in the group has a chance to participate, both in giving input and sorting the results. Take time to ensure that each team member endorses the results.

The Transformational Leader is responsible for making sure that this process is done, posted, and enforced. It will define the path to transform wasted time into productive, energized team productivity.

Get to know each other
Getting to know a person is getting to know what is important to that person. It is getting to know what his or her goals and dreams are. It is getting to know how he or she feels about ministry.

Develop a way to share goals with each other. Knowing what people are passionate about and knowing what their priorities are will help you in your work together. Working together is not just about what your current duties and responsibilities might be, but about who you are in God's eyes and what special gifts God has given you that you are using in leadership. Share goals in print. Take time to share results with each other and celebrate success. Take time to encourage each other when the going gets tough. Take time to review strategy when the goal needs to be refined. Take time to assist when requested. Take time to listen when emotions are stretched. Listening does not mean solving a person's problem or even commenting on the information – unless requested. Listening means listening.

Another Covey principle is "seek to understand before seeking to be understood." Care about what they want. Then, they can care about what you want. Here's another opportunity for listening. Listen and repeat what you have heard to validate that you have heard and understood. Do not think about your response while you should be focusing on what is being said.

Consider putting all goals for the team -- common and individual goals -- on a group calendar. This single step will do a tremendous amount toward building understanding and unity to the group.

Finally, make sure that you establish a regular time for team meetings. You may not need to meet weekly or monthly. Establish a schedule and allow for a called meeting when business arises that require action. Do not meet unless there is a reason. Make sure that everyone knows your agenda, both formal agenda and informal. Declare what you want up front. Model what the standard should be.

Create a team action plan – plan to celebrate
Make a list of tasks. Group them by project. Assign responsibility before the meeting is over. Define the completion date. Distribute copies to all members, even if they do not have an assignment. Time cue the deadlines in a group calendar. Set the standard for productivity and accountability up front. Plan a celebration.

Think about your work situation. How often do you celebrate success with your colleagues? Do you celebrate success as often as you complain about problems? Doesn't it make sense to have an equal ratio, or better yet, a ratio strong in celebrating and low in complaints? Find ways to publicly show appreciation for the team's success and for each member's recognition of achievement.

Care about the success of each member. Do not care about gaining credit for your own achievement. Build up the team as a team, and the team will validate your leadership.

Why is it so difficult for us to compliment our colleagues when affirmation is due? Take time to acknowledge the efforts and achievements of each person and give credit where credit is due. You are the leader. Treat others in ways that you would find encouraging to your energy creation process.

Transform the culture – care about your team members and show how you care.

Inspire a "team attitude"

The culture of team counters the culture of self-fulfillment – or does it? Value the team and each member can be fulfilled as the team is validated. It is important that each member make a contribution to the creation, development, and implementation of team projects and concepts.

Make sure that no single person takes the burden or the limelight on a consistent basis. Nobody likes a glory hog. The hog sometimes tries to disguise himself or herself as martyr or the team super hero. Nothing kills team spirit quicker that the glory hog. This is the person who takes on every project or task and overwhelms those not as assertive. Do not let things get skewed, especially if you (the leader) tend to be the one taking on the majority of the assignments. Let others have their turn. Let them contribute their gifts and perspectives to the endeavor. If you take on all the work, then what will they do? How will they have a chance to succeed and prove their capability? How will you have time to follow up on those things you have delegated? Balance the assignments. Take some. Assign most tasks to other team members.

Assign some tasks to sub-teams. There will be energy created in shared projects with a firm reporting date. Insist that sub-teams report and get the endorsement of the team as a whole. Assign complex issues to these sub-teams to quicken the process. The more people there are on a team, the more difficult it becomes to define issues and define a plan. Use sub-teams to accomplish more in less time.

Example of teams and sub-teams in action:
Multiple teams in the church environment can create conflict wherever there is absence of communication. In several churches, I created a planning process for scheduling fine arts participation in worship that involved representatives from other teams. Here's how it worked. At the beginning of a season, I held a planning meeting to schedule when each of 27 fine arts groups would participate in at least one of three regular morning worship services. Those present for this scheduling session included representatives from other programs involving youth, children, and others. This helped prevent inadvertent scheduling of worship participation during another scheduled group activity.

Encourage team members to put individual needs below team interests. Nothing cools team enthusiasm more than "killer statements" from an antagonist who only wants attention and proceeds to get it by contradicting the group. Insist on group attitude and focus on group interest.

In establishing your team, choose members with a variety of talents and perspectives. This will give a wider range of skills from which to choose.

As decisions are made and plans approved, ensure that each member of the team has a chance to endorse the results before adjourning. This is of major importance. "We will commit" can be one of the team guidelines. Passive-aggressive behavior begins where the environment is not safe to disagree. It also exists where individuals do not have an opportunity to affirm or deny group results. It is not beneficial for anyone to leave a team meeting and say "I don't agree with the result – nobody asked me for my opinion." This is the single most destructive thing for a team and is the first thing that will destroy trust in a team. Make sure everyone "buys in" to the decision. Make sure all changes come to the team for endorsement. Make sure all comments to the contrary are dealt with openly and honestly. Keep no secrets. All information is "on the table" for everyone to see.

This perspective is ideal, certainly. It is a worthy goal, even if achieved partially and/or incrementally over time. Tell it like it is, then listen to how it is with someone else. Disagreement is fertile ground for creative decision-making.

One of the key issues here is that group decisions and group changes build trust in the team and the process. If evaluations are scheduled as a part of each session and a larger evaluation annually, then the ideals will be accurate and process and policy can be amended as needed. This will maintain the integrity of group process.

Create a positive environment
Keep expectations in front of them and mark them off when accomplished. Validate accomplishments as achieved! Give prompt feedback on performance and conduct. Be affirming even when correcting behavior. Correct misunderstandings promptly. Record group input so that everyone can view the content and results as the process unfolds. Be fair with critique. Imagine that you will have a turn and would like to be treated in a reciprocal manner. Mark off items that have been completed. Use a BIG marker! Share lessons learned or new ideas with the whole team. Be an encourager.

Play together
Is work all that you consider doing together? Sometimes people will initially show you their true personalities when the focus is on having fun, not on their performance. Plan meals and social events together. Encourage every team member to attend. Make the

rounds and help each person feel at ease and relaxed. If the team agrees to work together, then they can agree to play together. If they do not want to participate, clarify the reason. Make it a part of the team covenant that you will support a limited number of social events in a year.

Learn to enjoy the uniqueness in each person and enjoy the differences. Learn to live. Learn to grow. Learn to enjoy.

It's not what you achieve, but what you <u>become</u> that is crucial.

A note to the weary and frantic: Don't be driven. Know the difference between being called and being driven. Drive the brainstorming to get worthy, unique ideas. Drive the focus of the meeting so that you will end with results. Drive the idea of win/win so that no one loses. But do not be a driven person that is trying to do too much, too often. Plan team strategies. Allow for time to live and let live. Plan time to build the team so that more will be accomplished without it all falling on your shoulders. Take time to save time. **So – DO IT!**

6. The "Members in Ministry" Team

Learn how to recruit, delegate, and motivate talented volunteers.

> *Leadership is the ability to get extraordinary achievement from ordinary people.*
>
> Brian Tracy

The Transformational Leader creates synergy and unity by empowering those in God's service willing to give of their time and energy in God's service to the church. The volunteer pool at most churches can be very large and very skilled, if properly utilized. I served in one church where the volunteers were called "Members in Ministry." A strong volunteer work force will not only help get the work done, but might bring fresh insights to the same old chores. They will also become advocates for whatever project with which they are emotionally connected.

Learn to be the leader

Leadership skills you employ in this area are important to the transformation of volunteers into workers, critics into advocates, and detractors into supporters. Learn to define, recruit, delegate, support, nurture, and facilitate. The Transformational Leadership model enables leaders to get the right people, tell them what is needed, let people complete their tasks, and celebrate the results. After all, professional leaders lead. If we did everything, we would be called professional doers. Leaders lead. This means getting out of the way.

If you have lots of volunteers, then learn to limit your time with those who are not as productive and give more to those who produce. Here's a chance to use the 80/20 rule. Spend 80% of your volunteer support time with the 20% of the people who produce 80% of the results. Gather the remaining 80% of the volunteers who produce 20% of the results into groups. Support them as a group, not individually. This will give you a major bounce on your results and free up enormous amounts of time. (This is the "Pareto Principle" named after the nineteenth-century economist who developed the 80/20 rule for business.)

Learn to recruit

The first principle of leadership is having someone to lead. This might seem logical. But it is very difficult for some leaders to ask someone else to do something. Looking back at the previous chapters, remember that relationship comes first. Once you have earned the relationship, then it is easier to ask someone to participate in a program that you lead. It is even easier to ask someone that you do not know yet. This is a wonderful way to develop lasting relationships, if you handle it correctly. So, let's recruit.

Recruiting is a skill, not a chance roll of the dice. Get to know people - what makes them tick, their skills and talents, and their interests. This sounds like the background work you did to create your vision statement, doesn't it? Well, it is similar. Recruit people who want to do something worthy. Recruit a person who wants to be invested in something that is consistent with your goals and passions. Don't recruit people who want to set up a power base and hold on to it! This is critical! Recruit people to help for a specific time and for a specific purpose, and then rotate people and responsibilities. This is a very important principle! This principle will actually help you recruit. People will say yes more readily if they know that they will not get stuck doing the job forever. This is one of the greatest challenges to overcome in recruiting; so clearly define the scope of what you are asking them to do.

Define the task for which you are recruiting. Tell the person how much work is needed, how much you anticipate it taking, and how long the commitment will be. The normal tendency is to downplay the commitment by saying something like "It will only take a little time." Don't cloud your reputation in future efforts by creating the opinion that you are not straight with people or that you are just giving them a "sales job." Tell it like it is! Be straight! They will appreciate you for that and even work harder than they originally agreed to do.

It is really difficult to take a chance on being turned down when you ask someone for a commitment to help. Assume that people want to help. They deserve an honest description of what they are being asked to do. And they deserve the chance to say yes or no. Be prepared for a "no" answer. It is better to get that answer than to have an uncommitted volunteer doing a less-than-adequate job.

All this may be difficult for some leaders, especially since the majority of church musicians and pastors end up in the "Introvert" category of Myers-Briggs. That doesn't mean that you are shy or even that you don't want to deal with people. It just means that you do well by yourself and are energized alone as opposed to being with a group for energy. People can take your energy. Knowing that fact, if indeed you are an introvert, then use your energy wisely.

The rest of us who are "Extroverts" in the Myers-Briggs, may have another problem. We may find it difficult to give the introverts the space they need to do what we have asked them to do. We extroverts may want to socialize and help. Remember, you are not recruiting a friend. You are recruiting a worker! Figure out their best style of relating and then delegate!

Learn to delegate
Once the person agrees to the task at hand, then arrange for a meeting to define the task. Don't do this in the hall or in the parking lot as you are going from place to place or from meeting to meeting. This will convey the wrong feelings about your

commitment to their success in the prescribed task. Arrange a time and quiet place to meet. Have something in writing to give them, which will define the task. Do this even if they say they know "all about it." Don't take a chance on any misunderstanding, which will negate the work they do. There is nothing worse than having to tell willing volunteers that they have done the "wrong thing." Well, it wasn't wrong to them, or they wouldn't have done it.

Another reason to clearly define the scope of the task or project in writing is to set limits on decisions that are made on your behalf or on behalf of the organization. Tell them what you want, and tell them what you do not want. Set limits at the beginning. Put it in writing.

Here's another principle for delegation. Delegate enough tasks to free up your time to follow up with those delegations. This is important to them and to your continued success in empowering volunteers.

Follow up your written conversations with written notes. Give the volunteer the task description at your meeting. Send a letter affirming what you agreed on, highlighting the final goal and how it will be identified and celebrated. Also, define ways for you to check on the progress of the task at critical points in the process. Don't delegate and forget. Delegate and support!

Learn to support
When was the last time you wrote a note to someone just to say that you care about what he or she does, acknowledging him or her personally? This is primary support for your team of volunteers. Write a note to someone every day. If you do one or two a day, you can manage the task and it becomes a habit for success. The response to this is worth it. Don't let this task back up on you. Do some every day. Take your days off, but do this on workdays.

Call to check on how the project or task is coming along. Just say that you are thinking about them and wondering if they have any questions or comments, or just wanted to tell you how it was going. You are also encouraging progress. Some people have bad work habits and will put off things until it is too late to do a valid job. Accountability is critical. You are accountable to them for what you promised – support and guidance. They are accountable to you for delivering the results as agreed. They need your support, even if they don't realize it.

Notice and comment on things they do and how they do them. We all want to be recognized for our accomplishments. Give them attention in positive ways that affirm their gifts. Keep your distance. Define how much time you will give to them. Set clear time limits. Affirming people does not need to create dependency. You need to budget time for everyone.

Staying knowledgeable and informed about their work is a good example of multi-tasking. Define, affirm, follow up, support, and celebrate.

If you are personally committed to a certain task, and you are not willing to let a volunteer complete a task in his or her own style, you should probably find time to do it yourself

Build teams and become the team facilitator
1. Choose the best skilled people available for the team.
2. Clarify the mission, vision, and goals.
3. Clearly define the area and scope of responsibility and decision authority.
4. Enable and empower everyone for excellence.
5. Stay knowledgeable and informed about their work.
6. Know each person, and be understanding of who he or she is and the work they have undertaken.
7. Be firm and assertive, but flexible.
8. Remain alert and involved, but unobtrusive.
9. Learn delegation; learn to live with group decisions.
10. Manage the details and the process as you lead people.

Fill in the details. Manage things – lead people. Set the pace. Set the example. Set the mood. You are the Transformational Leader.

Here are a few key words for your creative thinking:
- Recruiting – how to attain that "critical mass" to achieve the optimum

- Mentoring – how to empower people in your team to succeed
- Motivating – how to get others excited about succeeding
- Testimony – how to tell others what you believe
- Modeling – how the speed of the group is the speed of the leader
- Focusing – how to set realistic, attainable goals

So far you have been challenged to revisit your calling and insure that you are still on track. Insure that it is the track where God is currently calling you to appropriate action. You have been challenged to refine your goals, both for your job and your life. And you have been challenged to continue the life-long process of learning and growing as a professional.

Once you have gotten yourself together, then remember that you cannot succeed in a vacuum. Create the best relationships with those who surround you, both at work and in other places in life. The Transformational Leader influences everyone with whom he or she comes in contact with in one of three ways: positively, negatively, or neutrally. The choice is yours each time you relate to anyone. Which way do you want to influence others?

A note to the weary and frantic: This process of empowering volunteers is a bit frightening, isn't it? It seems as if volunteers just want to take over. Yes, let them take over, but give them a specific task they can complete in a specific time period. This will magnify the overall effectiveness and overall ownership of every program where they can fit in. So – **DO IT!**

SECTION 3

Effective Leaders are Transformational

*Determine that the thing
can and shall be done,
and then we shall find the way.*

- Abraham Lincoln

*Success on any major scale
requires you to accept responsibility...
In the final analysis, the one quality
that all successful people have...
is the ability to take on responsibility.*

- Michael Korda

This section deals with the music professional's responsibilities in areas that are not related to making music, areas that so often are detrimental to the overall effectiveness of the music ministry when these things are out of balance.

7. Getting Things Done

Choosing priorities and ordering our time

*A good leader is not the person who does things right,
but the person who finds the right things to do.*

Anthony T. Dadovano

This chapter outlines the principles of establishing and choosing priorities as well as adhering to those decisions. These priorities come from having a strong mission and vision statement. If we cannot order our time, then we cannot be constantly effective.

Why

Decide why you are doing every thing you do. Is it consistant with your vision and mission statements? If you do not really know why, then don't do it! Transform your life by eliminating unnecessary tasks!

Develop a reliable system

Develop a system and support for that system. Use paper or electronic means. Make a decision. Make a plan and work the plan. Have ONE calendar. Those who keep two calendars know that BOTH of them are usually wrong! Record all your data in one source and have a reliable back up! If you keep a paper system, attend a seminar on the effective use of the system. They will teach you the basics and then you can modify it to suit your needs.

The greatest help is to write everything in one system. EVERYTHING! When writing phone numbers or notes to call someone back, don't use those silly pink phone pads and have lots of little pieces of paper floating around. They are always in the way and you can't find the phone number when you need it! Scattered and disorganized people waste time that could be better spent in productive ways.

Don't take legal pads to meetings to record notes – use a meeting sheet in your calendar system. Time cue the action items on your calendar and refer to the appropriate page in your notes for the details. Your calendar page should have a section for tasks next to the times of day for appointments. Remember, only put items that require your physical presence on the calendar. Other items go on the task or project list.

Here's the basic idea. Record meetings in your date book. Record follow-up calls or actions in your task list. Connect the two in some way. Only put meetings that require your physical presence in your date book or calendar. That is a clear statement of where you are to be. Here's a good place to plan your personal time as well. If you don't schedule planning time, preparation time, study time, thinking time – then it most likely will not happen. Make a date with yourself and keep it.

Set a time of day to return phone calls. As the messages collect, put them into your task list for the time scheduled. The best time for calls is at the end of the morning or the end of the day. Do not interrupt productive time with phone calls, unless they are a priority. Plan your day the day before. Plan the major events of the week on Friday and review or refine and put in the details the day before, not on the current day. If you begin your day without a plan, much of the day will slip by without being productive.

Use your computer calendar program, PDA, or paper calendar system such as the Covey/Franklin planner. They have all the resources you will need and the training to go along with it. Keep everything in the system you use - phone numbers, addresses, e-mail, names, and other pertinent information. The beauty of this kind of consolidation is that you always have contact information handy when you need to follow up, and you can use extra time for planning or making notes. Extra time comes when you don't expect it, such as when waiting for a doctor's appointment or in the school line to pick up kids. By now, you've got the idea – now find a system and work it!

Transformational Leaders are disciplined and structure their time to get things done so that they have time to live.

Learn to plan ahead

You don't need to plan out your whole life in one sitting or even plan out the year, but learn to anticipate what needs to be done in the short and long term. You can plan several events at the same time and save time and energy as well. Set aside time to enter events into your calendar. Set aside time for study projects. Set aside time on a regular basis to think, reflect, and research. If you are constantly running full-speed ahead, then you have no time to get ahead, or to evaluate or resource your efforts.

Don't wait until things are in crisis. Look at the big picture before planning all the details. Make a rough outline, then fine-tune and fill-in the blanks. Make a resource list for planning so that you don't leave out anything. Assign priorities to every item. Choose a system, such as giving letters for priorities (A=Highest, B=Next Highest, etc.). Don't give every item an "A" or this system won't work. Do the highest items first, then go the next priority.

As you plan your daily schedule, consider priorities as well. Do not plan your day too tightly. Allow for sliding priorities – those things that are important, but unanticipated. If someone comes to visit who has a personal tragedy in his or her life you must be able to adjust your priorities so that you can deal with that hurting person. This is an unanticipated priority that must be fit into place. If you have planned your day with too much on your schedule, then something of value must be bumped. Bumping is fine on an occasional basis; however, if this is a normal routine, then it will undermine your effective and careful planning process.

If you have unassigned time in your schedule (dream on), then look ahead to the next day's or the next week's schedule and see if there is something that can be done ahead. It will be valuable to have some tasks out of the way if you have a scheduled task that takes more time than you have allowed. There must be a place to catch up. The other option is to reward yourself for being efficient. Learn from this – do not over plan.

Allow for creative reinforcement - time away from your normal surroundings to work on a creative project without the burden of the ordinary or the pressure of the workplace. Allow for creative space – both physically and chronologically – to recharge your administrative energy.

When items on your "Task List" are complete, then find a way to mark them off boldly. Celebrate the completion of the task or assignment! Don't mark it off with just a fine point pencil – use a big bold marker! Feel the success! Enjoy marking it off! Know that you have succeeded. You might think this is funny. Try it! See how good it feels! Success is not only intellectual. It is emotional as well. Enjoy!

Transformational Leadership begins with transforming yourself and your personal routines.

Your daily personal schedule should allow time for greeting people as you come and go. In arriving at work, leave time to visit with those whom you encounter on your way into the office. Learn to spend a little time with people so that you can cultivate a relationship with them, viewing people relationally and not functionally. Ministry is about relationship. You must earn a relationship with someone before you can impact what that person does. Give yourself room to breathe in your daily schedule.

Know your schedule and adhere to it
Have you ever missed a meeting because you simply did not look at your calendar? Certainly, we all have done this and regretted it. Use your calendar! Know how your day looks from the beginning. Know what needs to be done and how much time and energy it will take to do it. Prepare mentally and physically for the day ahead.

You have planned your day; now work your plan. If you are constantly revising your daily plan, then learn to plan more efficiently. It takes time to rewrite your plan every day. Now, please don't be too hard on yourself. Revising our schedules is normal. Undergoing a complete makeover means that you were not realistic when planning. Planning is not an automatic success. You will have to learn this skill as you have learned others. The essential point here is to keep on planning. You will learn as you go. Plan - read your plan - work your plan. It only takes a little time each day.

Knowing your plan also lets you know if you can interrupt the plan when others need you. Decide if their priority is your priority. The old saying is: "Lack of planning on your part does not necessitate an emergency on my part." Don't let those who do not plan constantly interrupt your plan with their problems. Learn to say no to interruptions that are not valid. Learn to tell others that you can schedule time later for them. Ultimately, they will respect this – or figure out how to solve it themselves.

Know what is important on today's schedule because if you do not get it done, then what is important today might become urgent tomorrow! Start your projects early enough to do them well. Don't get caught spending time solving problems that are unimportant or that have less importance. Give preference to important things and solve unimportant issues in less productive times of the day, before they become urgent. Management by crisis might give you adrenaline, but it might also give you more stress than you can handle on a regular basis.

Your carefully managed schedule allows you time for recreation and rest, for socializing, for personal reflection, and for time to enjoy your day. This is actually good stewardship. Learn to be a good steward of God's blessing of time.

Constantly evaluate your schedule
I repeat a very important concept - know WHY you are doing everything on your schedule. If it does not support your personal

vision and mission and the vision and mission of your organization, then why is it on your schedule? Evaluate the why along with the other factors of time, resources, and talent.

Know that something is on your schedule because you cannot delegate it or that it is important to your personal fulfillment of your vision and mission. If it can be delegated, then delegate it. Refer to the chapter on volunteers for ideas on delegation.

Do it now

Procrastination is an art, a fine-tuned skill, and a deadly mistake! When you open your mail – do something with each piece - NOW. Don't put it away to file later. Moving paper around in your office is a royal waste of time. Touch it once! Act on it – or discard it! Move on!

Actions on mail or notes could be handled in one of several ways:
1. File it.
2. Return it to the sender with your notes.
3. Discard it.
4. Pass it on to the appropriate person - with your notes.

Learn to plan; learn to delegate; learn to say "no."

A note to the weary and frantic: This process of planning your day may seem tedious and even a waste of time for those who have a clear idea of their objectives in mind. Well, there are blessings in careful planning. The Holy Spirit works quite well through careful, intentional planning. This is an area that has to be experienced to appreciate. So – **DO IT!**

8. Meetings, Meetings, Meetings

Effective Time Use and Building Consensus

Come, let us reason together. Isaiah 1:17-18

Don't you just love meetings? Everyone comes; some talk, some take notes, everyone leaves...and then? What happened? Most of us just consider meetings a necessary evil - a major waste of time! Meetings are also forum for power. Someone wins - someone loses. Sometimes, we don't even know WHY we are meeting! There IS a better way!

Being a conductor who must prepare for a rehearsal, I fell into an opportunity that opened my eyes to a more effective use of time when groups gather to make decisions, work out conflict, or formulate a plan. Some refer to this style of running a meeting as *Visually Displayed Thinking, Compression Planning, Creative Planning,* or *Visual Mapping.* But, for me, it is closely aligned to my skill as a conductor, bringing out the best in each participant and building a sense of unity through the process. The leader, in this case the facilitator, controls the PROCESS and the group provides the CONTENT. How great this is! I always hate going to a meeting where someone shoots off their mouth to get their way and the rest of the group lets it happen! Or, the group, with no clear directive, uses up the allotted time with no tangible result. The meeting expands to fill the allotted time, no matter what the agenda! No wonder we all hate meetings!

Let me offer you a better way, one that coincides with the skills of a conductor. Equip yourself as a knowledgeable facilitator, or hire an outside facilitator. In some cases, only an outside facilitator can achieve the desired results. If you have time to plan the process, do it. If not, hire an expert in process management.

Here's a definition of terms:

Facilitator – This person plans the meeting, leads the meeting, and remains neutral. Remaining neutral is central to the process. If the group feels that a facilitator controls the content, then it will not function effectively. The ratio of planning to meeting time is like that of a musical rehearsal. Two to three hours of planning for each hour of the meeting is the norm. This is a minimum requirement if you expect results.

The facilitator controls the process, the participation of members, and keeps the group focused and on track. The pace of the meeting is crucial to the creative planning process. Always stand, always look people in the eye, always listen carefully to exactly what people are stating, always try to involve each person in the process.

The facilitator also plans the design for the meeting. Notice I used the term "design" rather than "agenda." This implies that you've done more than write down some words on a piece of paper, gathered people, and called it a meeting.

The Project Team - This team may be one already in place. If not, then select a team that is not completely of one mind. For example, if you are planning a public musical event, then include a non-musical person in the process. Too many similar perspectives make a group blind to other tastes or opinions. An "outsider" or non-expert can sometimes allow the group to experience a paradigm change which could be most beneficial, not only to that ministry, but maybe to the whole organization!

Another important issue is that of enabling groups of individuals, with all of their individual perspectives and needs, to think and function as a team. Whether your facilitation is a one-time project with a team you've selected only for this task, or if you use these principles with an ongoing staff team, getting people to envision themselves as part of a larger entity is the principle goal. Work for the win/win situation in which individuals are fulfilled as the group's success is manifest.

The "Meeting"

The following points are essential to a successful meeting:

- Always start and end on time! Even plan the meeting for times that imply punctuality, i.e., 9:02 to 10:32 a.m. Promise to start and end punctually – and do it! Always!
- Seat the group facing the visual support, usually around three sides of a table with the facilitator at the fourth side. Some facilitators use chart pads. I use storyboards and various cards of various sizes and colors. With cards, you can have more flexibility. Print them with your computer and place emphasis on different items by using different sizes and colors.
- Appoint or seek a volunteer to be a scribe or recorder. Record the actions and ideas of the group where everyone can see. This helps the group stay on track, and reminds them of what they have created so far.
- Tell groups not to take notes. Instead, I send summary notes to them within 48 hours. This enables everyone to participate equally (if they aren't taking notes, then they can pay attention) and ensures that everyone has the same details in their notes.
- Ideally, the group should be small – 7 to 10 people. This allows for full participation from each person. If the group must be larger, then allow opportunities for splitting the group for discussion, brainstorming, problem solving, and other activities. When the group comes back together, each section reports on its results.
- If someone has a dominant personality or has a known strong bias, don't seat them in a dominant place. Choose a corner of the table. It makes a difference, really.
- Plan a timeline that includes each part of the meeting. Be conservative. Things take longer than you might think. Allow for a summary or debriefing at the end, or time to set up the next meeting.

The essence of facilitation is different than that of a meeting.

The essential parts are as follows:

- **Clarify** – Give sound, clear reasons for the meeting. People want to know WHY they are there and WHAT they are to do. Also give a time-line for the overall project. Is it going to take 3 months or just one meeting of two hours? Give the project a name or title, such as the title of a book. Choose the words carefully; they will begin to set the focus for the team.
  - **Examples:**
    - *Planning the Best Choir Retreat Ever*
    - *Building an Awesome Music Ministry*
    - *How to Recruit, Equip and Motivate Members in Ministry*
- **Define** – Prepare a concise statement defining the overall objective(s) of the team. Be specific. Then define the measurable objectives for the immediate meeting. Separate the long-term and immediate objectives as well as defining what will NOT be discussed at this meeting. Make the objectives reasonable for the time frame allotted.
  - ***Examples of Deliverable Objectives:*** (where to focus our energy)
    - *Identify 10 unique ways to attract new choir members.*
    - *Define 5 concerts that will pack the church.*
    - *Identify and prioritize all the tasks for the Choir Council.*
  - ***Examples of Off-Limits Items:*** (where we can waste time)
    - *Dwelling on past failures*
    - *Discussing all the fine details of each event identified*
    - *Picking on personalities of those not present*
- **Communicate** – Tell the group HOW the process will work. They need to know the total picture and how they are expected to contribute to the end result. This

is most important if each person is expected to contribute.

- o *Examples:*
    - *First, we will explore all the options for question (topic)#1.*
    - *Next, we will sort and prioritize those options.*
    - *After the group gives weight to the options, we will develop a plan.*
    - *All of these steps satisfy the first objective.*

- **Validate** – Determine the common facts about the subject and present them to the group. How many times has a group spent time debating something that was unclear from the start? Make the playing field level – give everyone the same data to begin. This will save enormous amounts of time. This could be called *Background Information* or *Givens* or *Common Knowledge Facts.*

    - o *Examples:*
        - *List ALL of the known facts about the subject.*
        - *Don't forget to identify the level of decision making ability this group is allowed.*

- **Agree** – Allow time for every participant to review the common facts you just presented, review the objectives for THIS meeting as well as the list of ways to get off track. It is just as important to identify what the group is NOT going to do during this gathering as to identify what they will accomplish. Ask if there are any changes, additions, or deletions to the common facts. Then ask if they are ready to proceed with the objectives for today's meeting. Wait for comment. If you have no comment, state that you will be moving forward by general consensus. Bringing the group to continuing consensus is an important guideline. It is much better to work by general consensus than to vote on issues. Make this your continuing goal.

Allow for this point to sink in. Bringing the group to one focus is crucial to building the team. Consensus does not mean that everyone always agrees on every point. Individual power must yield to group needs. The process builds the team. Eye contact is essential here, as well as a pause for opportunity to comment. Once the facilitator has determined there is general consensus, state the fact, looking at everyone. Say that, because of the general consensus, the group can move ahead. At the end of the session, ask again if there are any exceptions. Hearing none, or after addressing the comments, ask the group to keep faith with the team by not speaking contrary to the actions of the group when outside of the group.

Process builds team trust.

- **Prioritize** –Get right to the first issue to solve or first question to ask. Here's where the facilitator earns his or her keep! In planning the meeting, ask first what the end result should be. (The question to ask yourself in planning: "What do you want to walk away with at the end of the session?") Plan the meeting by addressing the objectives for this meeting, keeping in mind the big picture – the overall goal of the team. Therefore, keep it manageable by exploring ways to address the issue or question.
  - o *Example:*
    - *Set specific, measurable objectives.*
      - *Bad – Enlarge the choir*
      - *Good – 5 ways to increase numbers in the choir 15% in 3 months*
    - *Address the objective by having the group answer a question.*
      - *Ways to have people clamor to checkout our choir*
      - *Reasons people might be interested in choir*

- - *Possible changes needed to attract people to choir*
  - *Sort the ideas; pick the best 5 (or more),*
    - *Use sticky dots (price stickers) for participants to "vote" for their best choices*
    - *Use markers to "dot" favorite ideas*
    - *Use a matrix (cost vs. difficulty or time vs. importance)*
- **Focus** – This could be "FOCUS, FOCUS, FOCUS." The facilitator is in charge of keeping the group on track. If you have written objectives and off-limits items, then it could be as simple as pointing to those lists when things begin to get out-of-hand. Address side conversations and irrelevant comments as they occur. HELPFUL HINT: Purchase small bells and give each member of the team one of them with the instruction to use the bell if the group begins to violate any of the rules. Most of the time the group will police itself. Keep the group energized by varying the routine.
  - *Examples:*
    - *Divide into groups of 3 or 4 people.*
    - *Have each group bring back 3 solutions and present to the team.*
    - *Put a time limit on break-out groups (1 minute per idea expected.)*
    - *After a long period, have everyone stand, stretch, and change places.*
- **Formalize** – When finished with a brainstorming and fine-tuning, move the cards into some kind of order or priority. Figure out a standard of measurement (cost, time, difficulty, etc.) to judge the ideas. You can buy colored price stickers and let each person use them to vote for his or her choice.

One sticker for each ten ideas – this forces choices for the BEST ideas, and then the group's energy becomes clear to everyone. Bad or radical ideas receive no votes, so it becomes clear to everyone that they are less valuable ideas. After this process of sorting the ideas, you should have the makings of a plan.

- ○ *Example:*
  - Action Plan
  - Communication Plan
  - Next Steps in the Process
  - A Matrix of Options
  - A Plan for Reconciliation
  - And more
- **Review** – Give time for the group to sit back and look over what they've done, making sure that it all makes sense and is practical. Assign responsibility for any action items or communications, and schedule the next session. Here is a good opportunity for each person to take a turn in making a 30 second comment about what they've experienced in the session. This can prove to be most valuable, and will unite the group as they move on to their next event.
- **Follow-Up** – Be sure to check on all delegated items before the next session. Delegation does not mean you can forget about it. It means you don't have to do it, so you have time to check on it and assist, if appropriate. Be sure to send out the meeting notes and follow through with any other commitments from the session.
- **Celebrate** – When the objectives are successfully met, take time to celebrate. This adds momentum and gives belief in process for future projects. Remember, **you are a team**!

There are multiple benefits from running a meeting in this manner. There must be a major reward since so much preparation must go into making the process successful. After all, don't we want to make the best use of each day God has given us?

Benefits of running a meeting with neutral facilitation:
- Creates positive team building and bonding
- Builds trust through the consensus process

- Gives the team common ownership in goals
- Provides a safe communication environment (attack ideas, not people)
- The goal-setting process boosts the synergistic characteristics of the team
- Promotes an understanding of contrasting views
- Empowers the team to respond within pre-set parameters
- Gets things done

Types of facilitation projects and results:
- Long-range Planning = Long-term Goals
- Project Team = Action Plan
- Budget Building = A Budget We Buy Into
- Evaluation = Future Planning Resource that We Believe Is Valuable
- Schedule Planning = A Team Calendar
- Conflict Resolution/Problem Solving = Consensus

Running Meetings as a Transformational Process
The leader, in this case the facilitator, controls the PROCESS and the group provides the CONTENT. Plan the meeting.

Note: See Appendix II: Facilitation Design Worksheet

9. Publicity

Transform the Energy and Effectiveness of Your Programs

Yes, this subject seems to be unrelated to becoming a Transformational Leader. However, it is related. because we need people at our concerts and other musical events with which to share our ministry. The transforming process is that of becoming something, growing in some way, and learning to share those dynamics with other people. If we spend a large part of our time and effort preparing for a musical event or worship service and the attendance is very limited, then the experience is not fulfilling. We must, by virtue of our spirit of making music, share with others in a significant way. Therefore, the church musician must be skilled at filling the church for these events, or at least having a substantial number of attendees who are interested in our ministry. The principle is simple; it's one of completing the circle. The fulfillment in making music is having someone to share it with.

Decide on your market

Know whom you serve. Know your market. If you are producing programs, then know to whom you will present the programs and why. If you are simply producing programs that satisfy only yourself and your immediate support group, then it is highly likely that only these people will support such an event.

This is very tricky. You know your craft. You know what quality looks and sounds like. And certainly you know which options are available. However, have you considered the enjoyment and fulfillment of the attendees?

Let's use special church music programs as an example. Is it solely quality programming that people seek? Or is there an "entertainment" factor that enters into the picture? Well, reality sets in here, and it is sobering. People want to attend events that are entertaining. Now, this is certainly defined differently for different people. What kind of music is indigenous for the group you serve? Do you want to reach out beyond your immediate constituency? When you make your goal to do an event, say, in this case, a Christmas season concert with choir and instrumentalists and orchestra, how many people do you envision attending such an event? What will they expect and why will they want to attend?

There are many, many Christmas concerts and many, many potential attendees. Why will people choose your event over the other options? Why will people attend multiple events in one season? Why should they come at all?

If you can answer these questions, then you can begin planning the concert. Plan an enjoyable event where people will leave feeling they have spent their time wisely. Know that they will leave with the intention of attending the next time you offer such an event. Know that they will recommend this concert to everyone they see and invite them to attend as well. Create an air of excitement around the event. After all, if it is not exciting and enjoyable, why do it at all?

When planning your event, list enjoyment as one of your goals. Plan the event, plan the publicity, and plan all the support systems, such as rehearsals, budget, concert dress, coordination of visuals (posters, bulletin covers, programs – have a consistent visual image), and be sure to plan your preparation time for study and rehearsal. You should also plan a "time budget" in addition to a financial budget. Know how much time it will take for every item. Some calendar manufacturers sell meeting or project planning aids for your calendar. These are helpful tools in considering all the factors needed for an event.

How many times have you attended a really good event to find that it was poorly attended because of inefficient promotion? A common flaw for the overworked church musician is to leave out the promotion part until the last minute, and then not have sufficient time to do a thorough job of publicity. This is a major part of the event and must be treated as such.

The Transformational Leader knows that energy is created for all participants in a performance when a healthy audience affirms their efforts. If fine arts groups just wanted to make music, then rehearsal would be all we needed. However, part of making music is sharing the music with others. How much more empowered would groups be if they could share their music with a full house every time they offered a program? This is a transformational experience!

Develop your resource list for promotion

Media: Develop a comprehensive media list. This is quite a chore, but is worth the time! See if you can share resources with some other entity. Network with other arts groups or other churches to see if they are willing to share their media list. Offer to update the contacts and share the results with them. Contact the local chamber of commerce or arts council to see if there is a list for sale. It's worth paying for the list!

Here are the items for your list:
Media type (print, electronic, etc.):
Contact person or position:
Phone number:
FAX number:
E-Mail:
Lead time for information:
Special editions or programs highlighting arts events (with dates):
Kinds of information or programs they will publicize:
Preferred method for receiving information (E-Mail, FAX, etc.)

Make a list of types of media before you begin the information gathering process. Examples are:

- Daily newspapers
- Weekly and/or free newspapers
- Network television
- Cable companies
- Radio
- Magazines

Note: Refer to Appendix III: Publicity Checklist for a helpful form.

Next, put these facts into electronic form so they can easily be updated and printed on lists or mailing labels. If you are going to put a specific person's name as contact for the media event, then set up a system for updating the information on an annual basis. Don't count on him or her letting you know about the change. Recruit someone who loves to use the phone or e-mail to do this task during the same month each year.

You must also send an inquiry to each of your media contacts to get them to respond on the following items:

- Contact person
- Preferred method for receiving News Releases
- Comments on your release form and the completeness of information
- Any other important information

After all, you are helping them do their job if you provide timely and accurate information on a consistent basis that interests their readers/viewers/listeners. They will appreciate your interest in providing this information and will certainly appreciate that you want to know what is helpful to them. This is essential to building a relationship with the media in your community. This is very important!

It is even better if you have the opportunity to meet your media contacts in person to discuss these items. Get to know them and appreciate their challenges. If you can make their jobs easier, you can get better coverage for your events.

Develop a relationship with media contacts. After all, they are people wanting to do a good job the same as you are. When meeting with this person and asking for his or her help in publicizing your event, you must be willing to promise something in return. Here's short list of promises to start with.
Promise that you will:

- Always send them your information
- Always send your information on time
- Always return calls promptly from media contacts who have questions
- Know their deadline dates and the preferred method of receiving your information
- Always do what you say you will do

Finally, spend time writing a note of thanks to the media contact at various times during the year. Affirm the good things. Celebrate the success. The success is not only for your programs but also for the media; it affirms that people are responding to their efforts! Also celebrate the benefit to the community. You are offering quality programming – they are receiving the benefit.

Promote programs internally
The best market for your church music programs is your organization's membership. Now, the easy way to address this group is by simply putting an article or announcement in the church newsletter or Sunday bulletin and hoping people will show up for your event. Some will; most will not. They will claim to have never seen the information.

Getting the attention of every member is your goal. Ways to do this include the two methods mentioned above. However, be very sure that what you write sounds interesting and invites people to an event that sounds interesting. Also, allow time for people to get the event on their personal calendars, but not so far ahead that they will forget. There are several layers for this kind of notification.

Long-range notices and short-range reminders are the keys to getting noticed. Notify readers with calendar entries or quarterly program notices that the event is coming up (three to six months ahead). Give enough information to get people interested. Then, give updates of interest along the way, with a short feature about some element of the program or some participant in the event (two to three months ahead). Then, make sure that notices are posted for at least 3 consecutive weeks. Calendar entries and/or announcements for your program are great ways to publicize. Multiple impressions work!

In addition to this easy and logical method for publicity inside the church, you also have the following vehicles at your disposal:

- Well designed, attractive flyers and posters strategically placed
- Announcements in previous concert programs
- Announcements in programs for other church events (you must reciprocate)
- Billboards
- Newsletters for different groups (Sunday Schools, study groups, etc.)
- Personal letters of invitation
- Verbal announcements from the pulpit (please check with the pastor first)
- Personal printed invitations for participants to give out or mail
- Free tickets of admission (this makes it seem as though seating is limited)

The idea is to create a whirlwind of energy surrounding the event. Energy going out brings energy back in. Only send out accurate, high quality, printed material. If you expect your program to be perceived as high quality, then the promotional material must be the same.

A note to the weary and frantic: Publicity is not as difficult as it seems. You are an expert at your craft - why not add this dimension to your skill set? It will take some time to initially design and implement; however, once you've done that, it's mostly repetition! So – **DO IT!**

There are forms for designing your marketing at the end of the book. Design your own forms or go to http://www.hughballou.com to download a Word version to modify.

Note: See Appendix III: Publicity Checklist, PSA, News Release, and Calendar Announcement

SECTION 4

Be the Leader

By three methods
we may learn wisdom:
first, by reflection, which is noblest;
second, by imitation, which is easiest;
and third by experience, which is the bitterest.

Confucius

This section emphasizes that the music professional has great potential and great responsibility, indeed!

10. Professional Concerns

Act in a Professional Manner; Ensure that You Are Treated Accordingly!

Leadership is a combination of strategy and character. If you must be without one, be without the strategy.

Gen. H. Norman Schwarzkopf

Circumstance does not make the man; it reveals him to himself.

James Allen

Men do not attract that which they want, *but that which they* are.

James Allen

The role of the church musician is that of a professional. It is common for this position to be filled with a part-time or very part-time person. The term "Part-time" is largely incorrect, since the job, even though it is not usually a 40-hour position, is a major life-consuming endeavor for the musician. There is usually insufficient pay for this staff member to attain sufficient training in just what is expected as a church professional. The inevitable result is a less-than-adequate performance, or more correctly, a less-than-professional attitude. This compounds as the stress level increases. The church music ministry professional is, in fact, not always what the name might suggest. This chapter deals with those issues that lead the church musician on a journey of professional growth.

Know the standards for your profession

You have defined who you are, and your values and mission - now know the standards of the profession in which you work. Know the professional standards of conduct. There are professional organizations for your profession. Join one of them and subscribe to the resources that the organization provides. Most professional organizations have a code of conduct or professional standards of conduct, which will include how you act and dress and relate to others in your chosen profession.

In the church music field, there are several choices for the choral professional. These organizations are slightly different, but have similar features as well.

The various denominations have music organizations, such as the FUMMWA (Fellowship of United Methodists in Music and Worship Arts) for the United Methodist Church and PAM (Presbyterian Association of Musicians) for the Presbyterian Church (PCUSA). There is also AGO (American Guild of Organists) for organists and organist/directors and AGEHR for handbell directors. In addition there is ACDA (American Choral Director's Association) for choral directors in any organization and MENC (Music Educator's National Conference) for music educators. Each of these organizations has resources for guidance to the musician in the workplace. For example, AGO and PAM have a section for professional concerns, which includes a code of conduct as well as guidelines for churches employing musicians, complete with a suggested salary scale.

In addition to knowing the professional standards for your vocation, know the norms for job requirements and for other factors, such as continuing education and benefits. Be clear on what the position requires and how you fit into those requirements.

Study the position description for your job. Understand all of the expectations and implications. Know what it takes to deliver what's required. For instance, some of the sites mentioned above state that some positions require twice the time noted in the position description to complete the requirements of the job. In Kennon Callahan's book *Dynamic Worship*, he gives an outline for fulfilling the requirements for a single choir. The weekly time commitment, according to Callahan, is fifteen hours to support just one choir. He points out that standing in front of the choir on Sunday mornings in worship may be one hour in length, but to grow a strong, vital faith community, the director must put in the time and effort to grow this dynamic. For instance, he breaks down the fifteen-hour commitment into responsibilities, such as nurturing, mentoring, recruiting, coaching, and pastoral care, along with the normally obvious duties of rehearsal, worship participation, study, and preparation.

What the Transformation Leader does as choir director and pastoral church musician is multi-faceted. Every aspect of the job has multiple implications, not only in the life and program of the church, but also in the lives and spiritual journeys of those who we lead.

A carefully constructed position description is essential to clarifying expectations not only for the person in the position described, but also for those who supervise and work as colleagues with that person. Misunderstandings create tension, mistrust, conflict, and upheaval, and are due, in a large part, to inaccurate or incomplete definitions of expectations. Clearly define the boundaries and clearly identify the duties so that the road ahead is clear for creating momentum.

Have an agreement

If your employer does not agree to sign a contract for your employment, then ask for a letter of agreement stating the terms of employment and the items that define those terms. This letter should include the following items:

- Terms of employment
    - o Salary
    - o Beginning date
    - o Benefits
    - o Office and administrative support provided
    - o Moving expense reimbursement

- To whom you report
- Reference to official documents that impact your employment
  - o Position Description
  - o Employee Manual
  - o Other official documents
- Outline of any verbal promises or expectations
  - o Change in salary
  - o Change in office space
  - o Long-term growth expectations or goal implementation
  - o Other expectations that are not written anywhere else

Memories are fragile and perceptions of various leaders and committees can be very different from each other. If it is in writing, then it is clear. This is not intended to be a legal document. It is intended to give you a clear path to success with the necessary support to get there.

Review the chapter on goals. It would be good to define some goals in major areas if you are beginning a new job. Be sure that there is enough time to accomplish the goals and that they are reasonable. That chapter will give you ideas. You might also expect to receive goals from the organization or church.

How these factors are implemented and how your requests are received will tell you a lot about the culture of the organization you are joining.

Be professional
If you expect to be treated as a professional, then be one! Transformational Leaders transform the culture in which they live by setting the pace and modeling behavior and standards.

The first standard on which professionals are judged is appearance. If you want to be treated as a professional, look and act like one! How you dress doesn't dictate your behavior or that of others, but it does set the stage for presenting yourself as a professional. Now, don't think if you put on a suit that people will change any negative perceptions they have of you from the past. Everything works together. Successful people look and act successful

The next standard is to be there. Yes, be in your office when you say you will be there. Be present and actively participate in meetings. Be on time for meetings, rehearsals, and for the beginning of worship. Even though much of the work that needs to be done cannot be done in an office setting, keep some office hours and let people know how to reach you or leave you messages when you are not physically present in your office. Be there for the people you lead and work with when they have personal tragedy such as a hospital stay. Be there by following up on meetings or special occasions with a note of clarification or a thank you note. Be accessible to those who need your leadership.

Be prepared
Know the expectations for your job. Do your preparation for each item. Know that it takes 2 to 3 hours of preparation for every hour of rehearsal. Don't short-change that preparation time. Don't plan too many activities preceding rehearsals unless it is unavoidable. If you must go from event to event, then make a comprehensive written plan for each event, and then segue from event to event. Back up from the sequence of events and plan some reflective review time to prepare your mind and spirit for what's ahead. Those you lead deserve your best efforts. Take time to regenerate, reflect, review, and pray. It will make a difference. Transformational Leaders transform themselves first.

Prepare for meetings. (See the chapter *Meetings, Meetings, Meetings*) Prepare if you are the leader or moderator, and prepare if you are a participant. Know the agenda and know what is expected from you. Review notes from the last meeting and prepare your assignments or reports. It is good to have copies or a visual report so that others can understand and assimilate the information you are presenting. Understand what needs to be communicated, and do it. If you don't want your time wasted by others, then demonstrate by not wasting their time. Be a model for what you expect.

Be prepared for worship. Know exactly what your role is and what parts you will lead as well as how those parts fit the parts on either side of it. Know where you need to be physically and when you are to move into place. Know where you will go afterwards. Have all your resources with you such as anthems and reading parts. Even if someone else is to provide those items, have a backup. One day you will need it. Be prepared by having all the details and communications taken care of before Sunday. Leaving too many items for last minute fine-tuning makes everyone frantic and creates stress that diverts energy from your main activity: worship. You can also prepare for worship by arriving early enough to review details with other participants and to prepare spiritually with time for prayer and meditation. Find time to be open to God's spirit, guiding and preparing you to lead and to worship.

Keep your skills current
In order to be the effective Transformational Leader, your skill set must be at its best. Sure, you went to college and have sheepskin to prove it. So what! You must prove your worth every time you are in a leadership situation. Keep your skill set current and constantly strive to grow in some area.

Here are some concepts that can be helpful. You are probably doing some of them already.
- Attend continuing education events (such as workshops, conferences, college courses, or conventions).
- Lead a continuing education event -- you will learn more than those you teach.
- Belong to and participate in professional organizations.
  o Denominational church music associations
  o ACDA
  o AGO
  o AGEHR
  o The Hymn Society
  o Choristers Guild

- Read professional journals and books and articles.
- Write an article for those trade journals -- you will learn more than those who only read.
- Network with other professionals in your local area.
  - Consider local church musicians and worship leaders.
  - Consider area choral, handbell, and instrumental directors.
  - Consider ministers and educators who actively participate in worship.
- Develop a director's support group.
  - Share information, ideas, and struggles.
  - Listen.
  - Contribute.
  - Have fun.
- Develop an internal feedback group to help you evaluate your effectiveness.
  - Make it informal – people whom you choose and will speak honestly.
  - Give them input in advance for the feedback you are looking for.
  - Ask them for feedback on other items you may not have considered.
- Develop a collaborative tutorial relationship with a local professional.
  - Choose someone you respect.
  - Feel free to choose people who do not work as professional musicians.
  - Choose a time frame.
  - Reciprocate with others.
  - Be open to suggestions.

Motivate yourself
As Transformational Leaders, we are motivators, not only for those whom we lead, but also for ourselves. Others will pick-up on our lack of motivation even if we think we are hiding how we feel. They will know that we are not clicking. Constantly set a good example. Be the person you perceive, all the time.

Be aware that the attitude of the leader influences others. You will influence those in the choir by your energy level and by your enthusiasm. Lloyd Pfautsch taught directors that many problems in a choir are reflections from the director! The problems were directed problems! Eph Ehly is one of the best motivational leaders in any field. Ehly refers to choir rehearsal as "attitude adjustment." This concept is priceless! After all, who doesn't want to feel better after a great experience in singing together! You are the leader. Transform attitudes by your personal influence!

Your results are greatly influenced by the attitude that is present in the learning environment. Lively, well-paced, affirming direction inspires good learning and an active, appropriate response. If the choir is not coming through as you intend, look in the mirror for the problem and then fix it. Have a backup plan for teaching every lesson and every skill. You will most likely need a backup plan on many occasions. The leader's ability and intensity directly influence the group's responses. Stay in touch with your effectiveness – video tape your rehearsals and review them with a colleague or mentor. Be quiet and listen to the input. You will grow as a result.

Associate with winners. It has been said that we become the average of the five people with whom we associate with most. Choose those whom you admire and hang in there with them. Learn from them and keep your eyes and ears open for new experiences. Those who have learned and demonstrated those lessons by their success are worth emulating.

Stretch yourself out of your comfort zone occasionally, but not all the time. Try something new occasionally. If you don't think that you are good at speaking in public, then speak in public. Exercise new skills to know that you are constantly growing.

Strive for results. Nobody cares how hard you work if there are no results. (Well, your mother will care.) Those who don't succeed confuse activity with results. Set your sights on success, not on activity. Constantly (daily, even hourly) look at a summary of your major goals to remind yourself of your focus.

Share your talent with others. Teach a class on what you believe. There are many subjects, such as the place for music in worship or maybe the worship experience itself. Transforming a culture involves educating the members of that culture on the value, meaning, and history of what we do together. If you teach a class on worship and ask questions about why certain parts of worship are present, you will most likely find that a great majority of the participants do not know. Educating worshippers on the "why" in worship helps them be willing and able participants, accepting the fullness of what is offered to the community. This will not fix complaints. It will, however, connect many people to the richness of worship traditions and the value of many styles of worship, while making some complainers into thoughtful questioners. If we cannot thoughtfully respond to the educated questions of those whom we lead in worship, then we cannot be fully effective as worship leaders.

Responding to complaints is another area that requires effective leadership. When responding to a complaint, respond as if it were a request for information. Listen to the exact words that are spoken. Repeat the complaint, rephrasing in your words to demonstrate that you have understood what was said. And then proceed to respond in a non-confrontational manner. Do not argue. Do not challenge. Just respond. Do not react! Respond!

Responding can fit several patterns. Responding to a complaint by answering a question works if complainers do not fully understand everything. Maybe they are not aware of a crucial factor that would make a difference in their understanding of the subject in question. Affirming their right to have an opinion is key to connecting and winning their support. They will have an opinion anyway, whether you affirm it or not. It's how and when they express their opinion that matters. If you are confronted in front of a group, your response might be very different than if someone encounters you in the hall or in your office. Dealing with a single complaint in a group situation is tricky – ask them to see you afterwards and make an appointment to deal with the situation effectively. Private matters should be handled privately, not where someone is just trying to get attention.

Responding to complaints is a skill. We should not expect everyone to agree with everything we do. How dull that would be! We can have meaningful dialogue and disagree without harming relationships. Disagreement can add richness to life, and, on many occasions, enlighten both parties to facts and perspectives that were previously missing or misunderstood. So, listen, think about your response, and begin with an affirmation. Affirmations can be presented in many forms. One response could be, "thank you for asking that question." You can use this even if you hate the question. It gives you an opportunity to exercise your leadership skills. It is a teaching moment. It is a ministry moment. It is not a winning moment. Conflict and disagreement do not need to be harmful to us personally. Separate the facts from the person or persons – yourself included. If you are not taking the complaint as a personal attack (even if intended that way) then you can respond as teacher and leader.

Conflict and disagreement will always be with us, especially in creative endeavors. Learn to deal with it constructively as the Transformational Leader. The transformation comes as a result of your wisdom and self-control.

In dealing with complaints and complainers, try to be grateful that the person cares enough to talk to you about the item directly, and not behind your back. We want to encourage direct dialogue and discourage passive-aggressive behavior. Understand and communicate that resolving the complaint is not the only issue. Validation of the person might be the primary issue. The complaint might not be a major problem. Listen to the words to determine if the person is saying what he or she really means. This is an acquired skill and you will most likely misinterpret some complaints. But you rarely go wrong by affirming the person. That doesn't mean that you have to affirm the content of the complaint or the behavior, if the behavior is inappropriate or the complaint is expressed in an inappropriate manner or in an inappropriate setting. Remember, you are the professional. Professionals always attempt to do the right thing, no matter how they feel. This is a conscious decision.

This information on complaints belongs under motivation because it is potentially one of the most damaging to our motivation and self-esteem. Music making is part of the very being of a musician and is therefore a very personal issue. When confronted with criticism, learn to separate the item being criticized from yourself as a person. Learn to recognize personal attacks as such and move conversation into a safe arena with another person present. Don't "go to the mat" fighting for an issue that really isn't going to matter on your deathbed.

A note to the weary and frantic: Being the professional does not mean being insincere or trying to be a different person than God made you to be. It means being the best at your chosen profession that you can be. Continue to sharpen your skills to be a well-tuned instrument for God to use in ministry. Stay prepared, stay alert to lessons learned, and hang in there when the going gets rough. You can do it. So – **DO IT!**

11. Leadership

Becoming a Transformational Leader

Example is not the main thing in influencing others;
it is the only thing.

Albert Schweitzer

Do not conform any longer to the pattern of this world,
But be transformed by the renewing of your mind.

Romans 12:2

There are tens of thousands of titles that turn up in an Internet search for books on leadership. The concept of Transformational Leadership is present, but not acknowledged, understood, or endorsed. Knowing the power of transformation helps the music professional know just how important their influence can be.

Becoming a Transformational Leader

Transform means change. How does the leader inspire, enable, and empower others to bring change into an organization? He or she accomplishes transformation by encouraging, sharing, coaching, trusting, modeling, valuing, reinforcing, and many others. Being a Transformational Leader is similar in many ways to being a Charismatic Leader. The major difference is the focus of the Transformational Leader on working through people and not through one's own power.

The Transformational Leader produces through people. The ideal model for this is the choral ensemble. The chorus is inspired and enabled by the enthusiasm and charisma of the director/leader.

There is a shared vision because they are working from the same piece of music as interpreted by the conductor. They are empowered to produce to the best of their ability by the positive direction of their leader. There is constant nurture and encouragement, both verbally (in rehearsal) and visually (in performance.) The role of the leader is to model, as well as to inspire and encourage. Let's take these items separately.

Working through people
Impacting people's lives and moving toward a strong vision is what the Transformational Leader endorses totally. Maintaining the unswerving commitment to the vision and encouraging others is one of the key driving forces toward success. Music directors, especially, recognize that they are in the business of transforming people and their productivity. The other transformation that takes place is the key: transforming people's lives through their participation in programs and events.

Working through people is the foundation of this form of leadership. Respect for the individual and for who they are personally. Building a strong vision and continually selling that vision to participants is one of the key roles the Transformation Leader plays. And it is a role that is fundamental to the organic make-up of the Transformational Leader. The charisma and enthusiasm that the leader shows is the inspiration to those who follow. It is the encouragement that followers need when days are dark and the going gets tough. It's the light at the end of the tunnel when there is no end in sight.

The leader raises the emotional energy in the group by his or her level of enthusiasm and support. Those who will follow need a strong vision, a strong encouragement, and strong affirmations along the way. If there are little signs of success along the way, then the belief systems for those who follow will be strengthened.

Getting people to follow you to fulfill a vision takes strong leadership skills, good communication skills, enthusiasm, charisma, and most of all trust. If people know they can trust you, then they will follow a path that is not yet clear to them. They will follow, trusting that the path is clear to you, or that you know how to find the way to the final goal. This requires the leader to model the way he or she desires his or her followers to act. The group will learn quickly if the leader is sincere or not. The actions of the Transformational Leader must be the same as the spoken beliefs. These actions will speak louder than any words ever will. So, the leader must lead the way by acting in ways that fulfill the spoken and or written vision.

Working through others depends on empowerment. It also depends on a clear definition of the vision and clear directions along the way. If you depend on those whom you lead to follow this model, then empowerment is essential. Let go of things that others can do. Help them develop the skills to do these tasks if they do not have all the skills necessary. Build their skills, as they are able to learn. Encourage, nurture, coach, and let go. Let them put their personal stamp on the work. Use their ideas as they apply to the vision. Do not discount their contributions, even if these ideas are not exactly what you would have done. They will do it differently. Get over it. Delegate and transform. As they develop ownership in the project, they will develop their own momentum.

Be sure to reinforce good work and acknowledge results. Celebrate their contributions. If they do not have all the information, knowledge, or skills to pull off the objective, give them some of yours. Contribute to their success in any way that you can. It's not about your achievement; it's about their journey towards transformation. Your achievement is wrapped-up with their success.

Transformation is not an event; it is a process. You are not a dictator, you are an enabler, a coach, and a Transformational Leader. Those who have experienced transformation will impact the world in which they live, work, and worship.

Disciplinary skills

The strength of the leader sets the speed of the team. Model the type of behavior you want. Give your best – expect their best. Know what you want – know how to handle the situation when things don't go right.

There are times to reign in your staff, the volunteers you've recruited, and yourself. Remember how it feels when people speak harshly to you, so when going about this reigning in, don't be harsh.

Remember always that the Transformational Leader works through people. You work through people by enabling, coaching, and encouraging, not by forcing or with raw power.

Transform yourself

Continually sharpen your skills for proficiency and continually focus your devotional life so that you are the Transformational Leader transforming followers spiritually. After all is said and done, the end result should be spiritual renewal, spiritual transformation, and spiritually equipping people for Christian service.

Getting too focused on programs, goals, and strategies can and will keep a leader away from the main focus on the spiritual journey. Keep your focus on God's work through your work. God transforms people through the talents given to you.

Set and keep a daily routine for personal devotion. Read constantly. Listen constantly to God's messages in the readings, through others, and in prayer and meditation. God leads; we follow. We lead, and others follow. Don't let that chain be broken. It is through God's power that we succeed. Read and remember scripture that relates to following God and that relates to God's equipping.

Building Leaders

Get to know all the people in the group over which you have leadership responsibility. Know their skills and desires. Know who can do what task and who will likely want to do what task. Leaders must be an example of the traits they expect their volunteers and staff to manifest in their duties. A good leader must also know what to ask from people and where to assign them. Do not expect a duck to act like an eagle. All of the positive modeling in the world will not change reality.

Choose wisely, and it will make you happy. It will make them happy. It will make the church happy. And you will get more accomplished! This means asking questions and listening carefully to the answers. Do not make assumptions here. Listen carefully to your staff and volunteers, and ask specific questions. Consider giving people a choice of different tasks and see how they respond. Sometimes people will agree to perform tasks that are not their first preference if they have previously been affirmed by the successful completion of a task they do prefer. Leadership is about relationship and personal fulfillment. If they feel affirmed and you have earned the right to ask because of your relationship, then they will be more willing to do more for you.

Give attention to the things mentioned in previous chapters about giving clear directions and getting out of the way. After all, if you are constantly interfering, why did you delegate the job? They will be left wondering why you asked them to waste their time and talent if you are doing the job anyway.

Build leaders by matching tasks with a person's skills and desires, by giving clear directions, by giving all the needed support, and finally, by following up with support and affirmation for a job well done.

Surround yourself with successful people

This is a repeat, partially, of previous ideas. If you want to constantly improve your skills and your efficiency, then associate with people you admire or from whom you can learn. If you have trouble with efficiency – if you think that you waste time – then do not associate with others who have not learned to use their time efficiently. If someone is constantly trying to catch up with his or her duties or is constantly complaining about not having enough time to get things done, then he or she will most likely not be the person who can help you. After all, every day has the same number of hours for each of us. We must figure out for ourselves just how to use that time. Associate with people who have balanced schedules, who are busy, but who know how to organize their time and their tasks so that life is not constantly out of control.

Learn to grow by learning to learn from the actions of others who you admire.

A note to the weary and frantic: Becoming a professional who is respected as a Transformational Leader is a transformational process in itself. Take time to learn how it will take place. Take time to do the foundation building. Take time for it to fully develop. So – **DO IT!**

SECTION 5

Now What?

*I dream of men who take the next step
instead of worrying about the next thousand steps.*

Theodore Roosevelt

This section gives concrete ideas on continual skill improvement
and spiritual growth.

12. Application of Skills

Developing a Plan for Your Future Success!

Never...Never...Never...Never Give Up!

Winston Churchill

Don't let anything stop you.
There will be times when you'll be disappointed,
but you can't stop.
Make yourself the very best that you can make of what you
are.
The very best.

Sadie T. Alexander

Maybe you've learned some new skills and developed some new concepts. What can you do with this new information? This chapter encourages continuing improvement.

Keep your calendar current and available
A current calendar will not only help you keep up with what you need to do and where you need to be, but it will also help you look back at what you've done. It's very good to have this resource for evaluation and review. Store the old calendars in a binder for reference. Make notes that will be helpful during the next year when the same activities come around again. You can learn from each event – even successful events can be improved. So, keep a journal or log of important activities for review. This will save enormous time and energy and massively improve your efficiency. You will discover that your memory, even if it is very good, is not infallible. Learn from the past and move to the next level.

Your calendar should also have a place for notes on meetings and notes on tasks in process. Always have the calendar with you. It is amazing how much work you can complete in the few minutes spent waiting for an appointment or on some other occasion where you find an unexpected window of opportunity. Do not let yourself end up waiting with nothing to do. Successful leaders always have a task in process and can use unexpected time to their advantage.

Constantly collaborate with others

Most working environments have both a formal and informal communication system. Learn to add your own contributions to help with connections. Listen for information that will be a connection with you and another staff person. Network with that person to learn about his or her projects; see if there are any opportunities for collaboration and cooperation. There are many communications sent to the various constituencies in any organization. See if there is an opportunity for combining mailings for greater efficiency and more impact on the reader. Fewer communications with more information will net more attention and greater retention than many mailings with fragmented information. This is very different than the communications I wrote about in the publicity chapter.

Collaborate with others on major programming. If your church is large, then everything that is added to the schedule and every item that is changed, either in time or location, may very well have a domino effect with other programs and activities. If you are planning a program or event that impacts a wide range of ages or multiple demographics in the church, then see if there are other staff members who will work on your project team. Use a wide variety of talent. Use people connected with different groups. Combine skills and talents to save time and more effectively produce the event.

Constantly evaluate your events

Make it a habit to evaluate programs or events after they occur. Ask others who were in attendance or in leadership to assist with this evaluation. Make a visual format for recording the input. Do this promptly after each event so the facts are fresh in everyone's mind.

Use guidelines for gathering data. Make three columns for recording input from the group. Head the first column with "What Went Well?" or "Things to Celebrate," or some other header that will lead the discussion to identifying the key items for making the event successful. Do this even if you, or others, do not think the event was successful. There are most likely some good things to record. Having had an event that did not go as well as planned will make it more important to have some positive input.

Head the next column with "What Needs Changing?" This is a positive way to identify items or elements needing improvement without framing it in a negative way. List all the items that could be improved.

The third column could be one of several choices. One really helpful header is "Things to Add?" This is different from what needs changing. These are new ideas, not changed ideas.

A forth column header might be necessary if an event was a disaster. Head it with "Things to Stop." This may be helpful and it may not. If you had time to fully plan and execute the plan for your event, then most likely you will not need this column. Keep the idea handy, just in case.

File your evaluations by event title with your planning sheets for that event and cue your calendar for reviewing both of these documents before the event repeats again. This is more important if the event is occasionally repeated and is not an annual occurrence.

Learn to prune, strive for balance

Much time and energy is wasted on planning events that are either not well attended or are no longer meaningful in the life of the congregation. Know why you are doing an event. Know it is supported. Know it is meaningful, not only to you, but also to an adequate number of others as well.

If you find the process of planning and producing events is drudgery and less than meaningful, don't continue doing it. Don't prop up the dead. Spend your time and energy on worthy programming that will affirm you, your participants, and those who attend. If you are known for only giving programs of the highest quality and of rich substance, then people will respond. You cannot continue to do those things that are not worthy.

As Covey teaches in the *Seven Habits of Highly Effective People,* don't let the things that matter the most suffer by giving attention to things that matter less. He further says, "Keep the main thing, the main thing." Yes, if something is important, then give it due energy to insure its successful completion. You cannot afford to be distracted with things that matter less. Focus on more important things in life and do not let other things rob you of energy.

If you don't keep yourself from burnout, nobody else will either. When you get burned out, then you are not much good for yourself or your church.

Summary

This journey has been about how the church leader, especially the music director, can effectively implement transformational change into the culture by working through those under his or her care in ministry. It has included elements of organization, as well as ways to energize and empower others. It has also it has included ways to be the master teacher and role model.

Do not try to implement everything at once. Learn the principles and make them your own ideas. Develop your team!

This book has, hopefully, given you some new ideas and maybe reinforced the ones you already know and use. Live life with the abundance God has given you. Keep a journal. Live a life worth writing about. Learn to work hard and learn to live well.

Grace and Peace to you.

A note to the weary and frantic: Don't try to do it all. Prune and focus on the best God has given, and give to God the best of what you know and what you have learned in life. So – **DO IT!**

Appendix I: Goals Worksheet

Goals

The Concept

By writing down your goals and objectives, you will have an action plan for success. You will have a clear picture of what you want to have happen and what the cost and benefits will be. You will know where you are going and how you will get there. Focus on exactly what you want and go for it – with conviction and determination you will succeed.

Write it down. Goals not written down are only dreams. Write them down and move into action immediately.

Choose goals wisely. Goal achievement is one thing – what you become and what happens to you and your team in reaching the goal is another thing!

Share goals with someone who will hold your feet to the fire. Accountability is a significant piece of the puzzle for making goals work. Not only will you be motivated to complete the goal, but you will build greater understanding with others on what your priorities are for life and work. Someone who has been a critic may just turn out to be one of your greatest supporters once the intent of your work is clear.

Take time to think! Take time to plan! Take time to study! Don't confuse *activity* for *achievement*. Do not just *say* you will succeed. Don't *wish* you could succeed. Don't just *expect* the counsel of the successful. *Act* on the plan yourself.

The Goals Process

1. Clearly define your goal. Write it down in specific, measurable terms. Establish a completion date.

2. Identify obstacles to reaching your goal.

3. Determine who's involved in or impacted by your goal.

4. List all the activities or objectives necessary for reaching your goal. Group them in 90-day benchmarks if the goal is more than 6 months away.

5. Sequence all activities. Concentrate on a single step at a time. Walk before running.

6. Estimate the time necessary for each objective and total time for the goal.

7. Activate key activity dates on your planning calendar.

8. Begin action immediately.

9. Be persistent in your plans. Don't let obstacles or naysayers steal your vision.

10. Share your goals with your supervisor, or anyone else who you feel will help you along the way (maybe everyone listed on your goal sheet), or the staff as a whole.

Goals Are

S M A R T

Specific - Picture what the end result looks like. Know what it is so you will know when you arrive. Be very specific. The goal must be written down to count as a goal. Otherwise, it is only a dream, which can change with a whim. Identify the group or groups targeted and define exactly what result is desired. For example, increase the effectiveness of the XX class by developing a ministry outreach team that meets regularly and targets specific prospects.

Measurable - Set a measurable outcome for the end result. There should be no doubt the goal is reached because there is an exact, quantifiable target. For example, increase attendance by 20%, reduce annual mailings by 2; reduce budget expenditures by 10%, etc.

Accountable - If the goal has a chance of succeeding, then it must be shared. There is synergy in openly sharing a carefully articulated goal. The person or persons who help make the process accountable also make it possible. For example: if you mention the goal to someone who responds to you with doubt or ridicule, that's real motivation! (Don't let a spouse be the one; they are too easy on you!)

Realistic - Aim at a target you can really hit or have a good chance of hitting. There's nothing more discouraging than not being able to reach goals repeatedly. On the other hand, reaching the goal is not the only factor - it's the process that counts! Be careful in setting your goals because of what you become in the process. Aim for something important, and the journey will change you.

Timed - Another essential factor in goal setting is defining exactly when the goal is to be reached. Set the date and plan to arrive on time. Be sure to give sufficient time to fully develop all the aspects of the goal and set benchmarks along the way. It is discouraging to look way ahead and think the project is too big. Check off steps along the way.

My Goals
(Your name here)

Goal

Completion Date

Objectives (including 90-day benchmarks)

Relationships needed to accomplish this goal

Obstacles to accomplishing the goal

Benefits of accomplishing the goal

Appendix II:

Facilitation Design Worksheet

Define the desired results.

Choose the participants.
- Define the group size (ideal is 7 – 10).
- Determine the major players.
- Invite someone to help the group seek fresh thinking skills.

Develop meeting "design."
- Identify the overall goal.
- Establish deliverables for each session.
- Define areas where time could be wasted.
- Define all "commonly accepted facts."
- Determine what questions to ask the group in order to get the desired response.
- Define areas to explore (Brainstorm) and areas to refine (Prioritize & Focus).
- Prepare ways to sort the results to develop a plan.

Determine how much time is needed.
- Time each step and allow for the unexpected.
- Allow for gathering, greeting, and parting.
- Begin and end on time.

Plan the whole process.
- Establish who will facilitate (and remain neutral).
- Consider the "rhythm" of the session.
- Plan what to do if things get "stale."
- Have alternate questions in case some don't work.
- Prepare all resources well in advance.
- Prepare the room to be free of distractions.

Appendix III:

Publicity Checklist, PSA and News Release

Sample News Release Form:

News Release

Your Full Church Name Here
Street Address
City, State and Zip
Phone

FOR IMMEDIATE RELEASE

Title of the Event
Sub-Title or Modifying/Clarifying Line

Enter the most important facts about the event in the first paragraph. Give information on event name, location, time, date, and cost, if any. List something about the event content and participants. Present some interesting fact to "hook" readers so they will continue reading.

Elaborate on the participants and content. Give more compelling reasons for attending this event.

Use this space to identify host organizations or sponsoring organizations and other facts such as contact information.
Calendar Summary:
Event: Event Title
Sponsoring Organization: Who is responsible for the program?
Location: Where will they go for the program?
Time and Date: What is the time and date?
Other: Is it open to the public and without charge (or cost)?
For Information: Who is responsible (and the phone number)?

Public Service Announcement

(30 Seconds)

Your Full Church Name Here

Street Address
City, State and Zip
Phone

FOR IMMEDIATE RELEASE

Title of the Event

Sub-Title or Modifying/Clarifying Line

Begin with the most important facts about the event. Give information on event name, location, time, date, and cost, if any. Mention briefly something about the event content and participants. Present some interesting fact to "hook" the listener. Give more compelling reasons for attending this event. Use this space to identify host organizations or sponsoring organizations and other facts such as contact information.

(Read the copy aloud, timing it. Listen to the flow, knowing it is for listening and not reading.)

The following summary is for radio personnel in case there is a place for them to elaborate while on air.

Calendar Summary:
Event: Event Title
Sponsoring Organization: Who is responsible for the program?
Location: Where do they go for the program?
Time and Date: What is the time and date?
Other: Is it open to the public and without charge (or cost)?
For Information: Who is responsible (and the phone number)?

Publicity Checklist

Event _____

Date _____ Time _____

Media Type	Lead Time	Date Due	Complete (Y/N)	Release Type	Resp. Person
Newspaper	3 weeks			Release	
Magazines: 1. XYZ 2. ZYX 3. Arts 4. XXX	4 months			Article, Calendar	
Radio Stations: 1. ABC 2. BBC 3. CCC	2 weeks			PSA, Calendar	
TV Stations: 1. WAAA 2. WBBB 3. WCCC	3 weeks			Calendar	
Billboards	5 months				
Posters/Flyers	1 month				
Direct Mail	4 months				
Church Publications: 1. Newsletter 2. Bulletin 3. Bulletin boards	1 month				
Personal Letters	2 months				
Community Organizations	2 months				
Other Churches	2 months				
Retirement Homes	1 month				
Previous Concert Programs	As printed				

Resources

Running Meetings, Facilitation

Bens, Ingrid. *Facilitation with Ease! A Comprehensive Guide to the Practice of Facilitations.* Sarasota, FL: Participative Dynamics, 1997.

Hackett, Donald; Martin, Charles L. *Facilitation Skills for Team Leaders: Leading Organized Teams to Greater Productivity.* Menlo Park: Crisp Publications, 1993.

Hunter, Dale; Bailey, Anne; Taylor, Bill. *The Art of Facilitation: How to Create Group Synergy.* Cambridge: Fisher Books, 1995.

Justice, Thomas; Jamieson, David W. *The Facilitator's Fieldbook.* New York: AMACOM, American Management Association International, 1999.

Kaner, Sam. *The Facilitator's Guide to Participatory Decision-Making.* Philadelphia: New Society Publishers, 2002.

Rees, Fran. *The Facilitator Excellence Handbook: Helping People Work Creatively and Productively Together.* San Francisco: Jossy-Bass/Pfeiffer, 1998.

Tagliere, Daniel A. *How to Meet, Think, and Work to Consensus.* San Diego: Pfeiffer & Company, 1992.

Leadership/Team Development

Cordeiro, Wayne. *Doing Church as a Team: Launching Effective Ministries Through Teamwork.* Honolulu: New Hope Resources, 1998.

Covey, S. A. *The Seven Habits of Highly Effective People.* New York: Simon & Schuster, 1989.

Doran, Carol and Troeger, Thomas. *Trouble at the Table: Gathering the Tribes for Worship.* Nashville: Abingdon Press, 1992.

Hill, Napoleon. *Think and Grow Rich.* New York: Fawcett Crest, 1960.

Greenleaf, Robert K. *The Power of Servant-Leadership.* San Francisco: Berrett-Koehler Publishers, Inc., 1998.

Lencioni, Patrick. *The Five Dysfunctions of a Team: A Leadership Gable.* San Francisco: Jossy-Bass, 2002.

Maxwell, John C. *The 17 Indisputable Laws of Teamwork.* Nashville: Thomas Nelson Publishers, 2001.

Maxwell, John C. *Developing the Leaders Around You.* Nashville: Thomas Nelson Publishers, 1995.

Sells, James William. *7 Steps to Effective Communication: Person-to-Person Process.* Atlanta: Forum House Publishers, 1973.

Time Management/Goal Setting

MacDonald, Gordon. *Ordering Your Private World.* Nashville: Oliver Nelson, Division of Thomas Nelson Publishers, 1985.

MacKenzie, R. Alec. *The Time Trap: How to Get More Done in Less Time.* New York: McGraw-Hill, 1975.

Newberry, Tommy. *Success Is Not An Accident: Change Your Choices, Change Your Life.* Decatur, GA: Looking Glass Books, 1999.

Rohn, Jim. *Seven Strategies for Wealth and Happiness.* Rocklin, CA: Prima Publishing & Communications, 1986.

Musicanship

Cameron, Julia. *The Artist's Way: A Spiritual Path to Higher Creativity.* New York: Jeremy P. Tarcher/Putman, 1992.

Garretson, Robert L. *Choral Music: History, Style, and Performance Practice.* Englewood Cliffs, NJ: Prentice-Hall, 1993.

Jordan, James. *Evoking Sound: Fundamentals of Choral Conducting and Rehearsing.* Chicago: GIA Publications, 1996.

Jordan, James. *The Musician's Soul.* Chicago: GIA Publications, 1999.

Page, Sue Ellen. *Hearts and Hands and Voices: Growing in Faith Through Choral Music*. Tarznan, CA: H. T. FitzSimmons Company, 1995.

Worship Planning

Dawn, Marva J. *A Royal "Waste" of Time: The Splendor of Worshiping God and Being Church for the World*. Grand Rapids: William B. Eerdmans Publishing Company, 1999.

Lathrop, Gordon W. *Holy Things: A Liturgical Theology*. Minneapolis: Fortress Press, 1998.

Saliers, Don E. *Worship and Spirituality*. Akron, OH: OSL Publications, 1996.

Saliers, Don E. *Worship as Theology: Foretaste of Glory Divine*. Nashville: Abingdon Press, 1994.

White, James F. *Sacraments as God's Self Giving: Sacramental Practice and Faith*. Nashville: Abingdon Press, 1983.

Spiritual Development

Allen, James. *As A Man Thinketh*. Marina del Rey, CA: DeVorss & Company.

Bonhoeffer, Dietrich. *Life Together: A Discussion of Christian Fellowship*. New York: Harper & Rowe Publishers, Inc., 1954.